## *Thoughts On Living A Happy and Successful Life*

**Todd Leigh Mayo**

**Pinnacle Press™ ◆ Sarasota, Florida**

# Words To Live By
## Thoughts On Living A Happy and Successful Life

Todd Leigh Mayo

Published by:
Pinnacle Press™
P.O. Box 2787
Sarasota, FL 34230-2787 USA
Phone: (800) 307-0001 Fax: (941) 953-3915


Printed in the United States of America

Library of Congress Cataloging-In-Publication Data
Mayo, Todd Leigh 1959-
Words To Live By...Thoughts on Living a Happy and Successful Life.
Includes Index
1. Self Help 2. Inspirational 3. Personal Development 4. Motivational 5. Gift 6. Quotations
I. Title
Library of Congress Catalog Card Number: 95-70414
ISBN 0-9647700-0-8 : $9.95
Cover design/illustrations by Lightbourne Images

# Dedication

This book is dedicated to my grandmother and grandfather for their lifelong unconditional support; for the values and qualities instilled; for their guidance, love and understanding. Without them, I would have never achieved this level of success. I thank them for showing me that the true meaning of success is giving to others, whether it is time, knowledge, support, money, whatever you can give. Their lessons will live on forever.

# Acknowledgment

So many people influenced this book that it would be impossible to mention all of them. I would like to give special thanks to Shelly Stewart for her hard work and patience, Elmer Lerner for his guidance and direction, Lisa Bashford for setting me free, and to all my family and friends who I treasure every day. I would like to especially thank my grandparents, Horace and Velma Mayo, who taught me the true meaning of happiness and success.

# Preface

Throughout our lives each of us has dreams or goals we want to fulfill. Sometimes it can be difficult to realize them unless we have some guidance. We need knowledge, enthusiasm, strength and motivation. We need to take control of our destinies and learn to live each day to its fullest while achieving the things we want from life.

This book is about being aware that there are no limits to your potential for happiness, growth, confidence, success and everything else important in your life. The philosophies in this book will help you reach the highest peak of human development and fulfillment.

I began collecting quotes for *"Words to Live By"* at 15 years of age. Whenever a new one was discovered, it became an added inspiration to find the multitude of motivational secrets as shared by others.

# Preface cont...

The ability to live our dreams is limitless. This book will help you develop a different way of looking at yourself and the world, and will inspire you to experience your ambitions.

I have been studying human behavior since the 1970's. Our companies (The Center for Self Improvement™ & The Foundation for Human Achievement™) specialize in researching and analyzing the habits, philosophies and attitudes of the world's most successful leaders in all walks of life.

Pinnacle Financial Advisors, another one of our companies, is engaged in the study of behavioral finance. This includes market psychology, personal risk tolerance, the effect of finance on personal relationships and analysis of attributes required for success in the business and investment world.

*"Words to Live By"* is a compilation of the actual principles, philosophies and attitudes

# Preface cont...

espoused by the many successful renowned individuals of the past and present. This is *a manual for living.* I refer to it frequently and use it to guide, motivate and steer me in the proper direction. None of us live perfect lives. We all need support and advice from time to time. *"Words to Live By"* should be a regular part of your routine whenever you need inspiration for success.

The following pages are full of valuable advice on success planning, relationships, communication skills, happiness, motivation, courage, risk taking, overcoming fears and obstacles and many other topics that will enhance your life each and every day. The individuals quoted in *"Words to Live By"* are the world's greatest achievers. Learn from their examples and choose greatness for yourself. Set aside your emotional barriers and free your mind to enjoy life to its fullest. I hope you enjoy reading *"Words to Live By"* as much as I enjoyed bringing it to you. ◆

Somebody should tell us, right at the start of our lives, that we are dying. Then we might live life to the limit every minute of every day. "Do it!" I say. Whatever you want to do, do it now! There are only so many tomorrows.

-Michael Landon

It is one of the most beautiful compensations of this life that no man can sincerely try to help another without helping himself.

-Ralph Waldo Emerson

Remember that discouragement comes from within.

-Anonymous

When you counsel someone, you should appear to be reminding him of something he had forgotten, not of the light he was unable to see.

-Baltasar Gracian

Failure is only a temporary change in direction to set you straight for your next success.

-Denis Waitley

The great Edison failed ten thousand times before he made the incandescent light work. Do not become discouraged and *quit* if you fail once or twice before making your plans work.

-Anonymous

Nothing in this world can take the place of persistence. Talent will not; nothing is more common than unsuccessful people with talent. Genius will not; unrewarded genius is almost a proverb. Education will not; the world is full of educated derelicts. Persistence and determination alone are omnipotent. The slogan *press* on has solved and always will solve the problems of the human race.

-Calvin Coolidge

Nothing splendid has ever been achieved except by those who dared believe that something inside of them was superior to circumstance.

-Bruce Barton

Fear not for the future, weep not for the past.

-Shelley

Too many people are thinking of security instead of opportunity. They seem more afraid of life than death.
-James F. Byrnes

First acquire patience and perseverance. Then, whatever else you want you will be sure to get it.
-Anonymous

Watch your thoughts; they become words. Watch your words; they become actions. Watch your actions; they become habits. Watch your habits; they become character. Watch your character; it becomes your destiny.
-Frank Outlaw

The sincere alone can recognize sincerity.
-Thomas Carlyle

Prosperity is a great teacher; adversity is a greater one. Possession pampers the mind; privation trains and strengthens it.
-William Hazlitt

The individual must control the deepest perception of himself lest he be overwhelmed by the forces of negativism and defeatism in the weaker individuals around him.

-Anonymous

If one advances confidently in the direction of their dreams and endeavors to lead a life which they have imagined, they will meet with a success unexpected in common hours.

-Henry David Thoreau

Reflect upon your present blessings, of which every man has plenty; not on your past misfortunes, of which all men have some.

-Charles Dickens

Find something you love to do and you will never have to work a day in your life.

-Harvey MacKay

They who forgive most, shall be most forgiven.

-Josiah W. Bailey

The credit belongs to those who are actually in the arena who strive valiantly; who know the great enthusiasms, the great devotions and spend themselves in a worthy cause; who at best, know the triumph of high achievement; and who, at the worst, if they fail, fail while daring greatly, so that their place shall never be with those cold and timid souls who know neither victory nor defeat.

-Theodore Roosevelt

The educated man is the man who has learned how to get everything he needs without violating the rights of his fellow man.

-Anonymous

Do not bite at the bait of pleasure till you know there is no hook beneath it.

-Thomas Jefferson

The difference between a successful person and others is not a lack of strength, not a lack of knowledge, but rather in a lack of will.

-Vincent T. Lombardi

The longer I live, the more I realize the impact of attitude on life. Attitude, to me, is more important than facts. It is more important than the past, than education, than money, than circumstances, than failures, than successes, than what other people think or say or do. It is more important than appearance, giftedness or skill. It will make or break a company, a church, a home. The remarkable thing is, we have a choice every day regarding the attitude we will embrace for that day. We cannot change our past. We cannot change the fact that people will act in a certain way. We cannot change the inevitable. The only thing we can do is play on the one string we have, and that is our attitude. I am convinced that life is 10% what happens to me and 90% how I react to it. And so it is with you. We are in charge of our attitudes.

-Charles Swindell

The essential element in personal magnetism is a consuming sincerity, an overwhelming faith in the importance of the work one has to do.

-Bruce Barton

Our best friends and our worst enemies are our thoughts. A thought can do us more good than a doctor or a banker or a faithful friend. It can also do us more harm than a brick.

-Dr. Frank Crane

Do not *tell* the world what you can do, *show* it.

-Anonymous

Lack of something to feel important about is almost the greatest tragedy a man may have.

-Dr. Arthur E. Morgan

The man who will use his skill and constructive imagination to see how much he can give for a dollar, instead of how little he can give for a dollar, is bound to succeed.

-Henry Ford

Most of us have a pretty clear idea of the world we want. What we lack is an understanding of how to go about getting it.

-Hugh Gibson

No man can become a great leader of men unless he has the milk of human kindness in his own heart and leads by suggestion and kindness, rather than by force.

-Anonymous

Goodwill to others is constructive thought. It helps build you up. It is good for your body. It makes your blood purer, your muscles stronger and your whole form more symmetrical in shape. It is the real elixir of life. The more such thought you attract to you, the more life you will have.

-Prentice Mulford

Fear not that thy life shall come to an end, but rather fear that it shall never have a beginning.

-Cardinal Newman

Nothing is ever lost by courtesy. It is the cheapest of the pleasures; costs nothing and conveys much. It pleases him who gives and him who receives, and thus, like mercy, is twice blessed.

-Erastus Wiman

I believe that diversity is a part of the natural order of things; as natural as the trillion shapes and shades of the flowers of spring or the leaves of autumn. I believe that diversity brings new solutions to an ever-changing environment and that sameness is not only uninteresting, but limiting. To deny diversity is to deny life with all its richness and manifold opportunities. Thus I affirm my citizenship in a world of diversity and, with it, the responsibility to: *be tolerant, live and let live.* Understand that those who cause no harm should not be feared, ridiculed or harmed even if they are different. Look for the best in others. Be just in my dealings with poor and rich, weak and strong and, whenever possible, to defend the young, the old, the frail, the defenseless. Be kind, remembering how fragile the human spirit is. Live the examined life, subjecting my motives and actions to the scrutiny of mind and heart, so to rise above prejudice and hatred. Care.

-Gene Greissman

There is no security on this earth. Only opportunity.

-Douglas Mac Arthur

The most unproductive, empty, fruitless fellow in the world is the man with a barren heart. Happiness can never reach him, for nothing good and lasting can lodge in his heart; it is solid as a billiard ball. Contrast this man, with his barren heart, with the human that plays the game of life fairly and honestly and is willing to make others happy by his own sacrifices.

-F.D. Van Amburgh

Circumstances are the rulers of the weak; they are but the instruments of the wise.

-Samuel Lover

Great men suffer hours of depression through introspection and self-doubt. That is why they are great. That is why you will find modesty and humility the characteristics of such men.

-Bruce Barton

Your only limitations are the ones you set up in your own mind.

-Anonymous

Regret is an appalling waste of energy. You can't build on it; it's only good for wallowing in.

-Katherine Mansfield

I wonder if the human touch, which people have, is not one of the greatest assets that one can have. You meet some people and immediately, you feel their warmth of mind or heart. You read a book, sit before the performance of a fine actor or read a poem and there it is, something that streams into your consciousness. Those who keep climbing higher in their chosen work, all have this outstanding something. The nurse in the hospital, the man who delivers your mail, the clerk behind many a store counter and the effective minister or public speaker. Without this human touch, hope has little on which to feed or thrive.

-George Matthew Adams

When you do not know what to do or which way to turn, smile. This will relax your mind and let the sunshine of happiness into your soul.

-Anonymous

The difficulties, hardships and trials of life, the obstacles one encounters on the road to fortune are positive blessings. They knit the muscles more firmly and teach self-reliance. Peril is the element in which power is developed.

-William Matthews

No one is rich enough to do without a neighbor.

-Danish Proverb

Worry is evidence of an ill-controlled brain; it is merely a stupid waste of time in unpleasantness. If men and women practiced mental calisthenics as they do physical calisthenics, they would purge their brains of this foolishness.

-Arnold Bennett

Money may be the husk of many things, but not the kernel. It brings you food, but not appetite; medicine, but not health; acquaintances, but not friends; servants, but not faithfulness; days of joy, but not peace or happiness.

-Henrik Ibsen

Three things too much and three too little are pernicious to man: to speak much and know little; to spend much and have little; to presume much and be worth little.

-Miguel de Cervantes

The greater the obstacle, the more glory in overcoming it.

-Moliere

Cherish your visions and your dreams as they are the children of your soul; the blueprints of your ultimate achievements.

-Anonymous

Small kindnesses, small courtesies, small considerations habitually practiced in our social intercourse, give a greater charm to the character than the display of great talent and accomplishments.

-Kelty

The man of decision cannot be stopped.

-Anonymous

Getters generally don't get happiness; givers get it. You simply give to others a bit of yourself; a thoughtful act, a helpful idea, a word of appreciation, a lift over a rough spot, a sense of understanding, a timely suggestion. You take something out of your mind, garnished in kindness out of your heart and put it into the other fellow's mind and heart.

-Charles H. Burr

Live your life each day as you would climb a mountain. An occasional glance toward the summit keeps the goal in mind, but many beautiful scenes are to be observed from each new vantage point. Climb slowly, steadily, enjoying each passing moment; and the view from the summit will serve as a fitting climax for the journey.

-Harold V. Melchert

Every failure is a blessing in disguise providing it teaches some needed lesson one could not have learned without it. Most so-called failures are only temporary defeats.

-Anonymous

It takes but a second to administer a rebuke, but it takes a lifetime for the one who has been rebuked to forget it.

-Anonymous

Wisdom is the right use of knowledge. To know is not to be wise. Many men know a great deal and are all the greater fools for it. There is no fool so great a fool as a knowing fool. But to know how to use knowledge is to have wisdom.

-Charles Haddon Spurgeon

Sincerity is impossible unless it pervades the whole being, and the pretense of it saps the very foundation of character.

-James Russell Lowell

Do not run after happiness, but seek to do good and you will find that happiness will run after you. The day will dawn full of expectation, the night will fall full of repose. This world will seem a very good place and the world to come a better place still.

-James Freeman Clarke

The ability to keep a cool head in an emergency, maintain poise in the midst of excitement and to refuse to be stampeded are true marks of leadership.

-R. Shannon

The most important single influence in the life of a person is another person. We may say to our children, "Here is art, science, philosophy, mathematics, music, psychology, history, religion." And we may open innumerable doors along the corridors of living so that they will have a broad and even a minute acquaintance with the segments of life; but these introductions are not as important as knowing people whose characters andactions, personalities and words have grown after similar introductions and have become worthy of emulation.

-Paul D. Shafer

Ultimately, nothing matters very much. The defeat that seems to break your heart today will be but a ripple among the waves of other experiences in the ocean of your life.

-Anonymous

*What is Teamwork?* Teamwork is the ability to work together toward a common vision; the ability to direct individual accomplishment toward organizational objectives. It is the fuel that allows common people to attain uncommon results. Simply stated, it is less me and more we.

-Anonymous

You can do what you want to do, accomplish what you want to accomplish, attain any reasonable objective you may have in mind. Not all of a sudden, perhaps, not in one swift and sweeping act of achievement, but you can do it gradually, day by day and play by play, if you want to do it, if you will to do it, if you work to do it over a sufficiently long period of time.

-William E. Holler

Get over the idea that only children should spend their time in study. Be a student so long as you still have something to learn, and this will mean all your life.

-Henry L. Doherty

The long span of the bridge of your life is supported by countless cables called habits, attitudes and desires. What you do in life depends upon what you are and what you want. What you get from life depends upon how much you want it; how much you are willing to work and plan and cooperate and use your resources. The long span of the bridge of your life is supported by countless cables that you are spinning now, and that is why today is such an important day. Make the cables strong!

-L.G. Elliott

The mere lapse of years is not life. To eat, to drink and sleep, to be exposed to darkness and the light, to pace around in the mill of habit and turn thought into an instrument of trade, this is not life. Knowledge, truth, love, beauty, goodness, faith alone can give vitality to the mechanism of existence.

-James Martineau

We have committed the Golden Rule to memory. Let us now commit it to life.

-Edwin Markham

The journey of a thousand miles starts with a single step.
-Chinese Proverb

Kind words do not cost much. They never blister the tongue or lips. Mental trouble was never known to arise from such quarters. Though they do not cost much, yet they accomplish much. They make other people good-natured. They also produce their own image on men's souls, and a beautiful image it is.
-Blaise Pascal

If you want something to happen, make it happen.
-Anonymous

Fear less, hope more; eat less, chew more; whine less, breathe more; talk less, say more; hate less, love more; and all good things are yours.
-Swedish Proverb

Most people are about as happy as they make up their minds to be.
-Abraham Lincoln

Render more service than that for which you are paid and you will soon be paid for more than you render. This is *The law of increasing returns.*

-Napoleon Hill

A pessimist is one who makes difficulties of his opportunities; an optimist is one who makes opportunities of his difficulties.

-Reginald B. Mansell

Life is a series of experiences, each one of which makes us bigger even though sometimes it is hard to realize this. For the world was built to develop character and we must learn that the setbacks and grieves which we endure help us in our marching onward.

-Henry Ford

Character cannot be developed in ease and quiet. Only through the experiences of trial and suffering can the soul be strengthened, vision cleared, ambition inspired and success achieved.

-Anonymous

A man's treatment of money is the most decisive test of his character: how he makes it and how he spends it.

-James Moffatt

What disturbs men's minds is not events, but their judgments on events.

-Anonymous

The worst sorrows in life are not in its losses and misfortune, but its fears.

-Arthur Christopher Benson

You cannot antagonize and influence at the same time.

-J.S. Knox

To live in hearts we leave behind is not to die.

-Joseph Campbell

Restlessness and discontent are the first necessities of progress.

-Thomas A. Edison

A man without a plan is not a man.
-Anonymous

If you can't get enthusiastic about your work, it's time to get alarmed, something is wrong. Compete with yourself, set your teeth and dive into the job of breaking your own record. No one keeps up his enthusiasm automatically. Enthusiasm must be nourished with new actions, new aspirations, new efforts, new vision. It is one's own fault if his enthusiasm is gone; he has failed to feed it. If you want to turn hours into minutes, renew your enthusiasm.
-Papyrus

When you hire people who are smarter than you are, you prove you are smarter than they are.
-R. H. Grant

Vacillating people seldom succeed. They seldom win the solid respect of their fellows. Successful men and women are very careful in reaching decisions and very persistent and determined in action thereafter.
-L.G. Elliott

You can preach a better sermon with your life than with your lips.

-Oliver Goldsmith

Rule #1: Don't sweat the small stuff.
Rule #2: It's all small stuff.

-Anonymous

People who cannot find time for recreation are obliged sooner or later to find time for illness.

-John Wanamaker

Whenever you are too selfishly looking out for your own interest, you have only one person working for you, yourself. When you help a dozen other people with their problems, you have a dozen people working with you.

-William B. Given, Jr.

The trouble with worrying so much about your *security* in the future is that you feel so insecure in the present.

-Harlan Miller

Nobody grows old by merely living a number of years. People grow old only by deserting their ideals. Years wrinkle the face, but to give up enthusiasm wrinkles the soul. Worry, doubt, self-interest, fear, despair: these are the long, long years that bow the head and turn the growing spirit back to dust.

-Watterson Lowe

We cannot consider people truly educated if they think of education only as the gathering of facts, data and information. The intelligent person is one who has learned how to choose wisely and, therefore, has a sense of values, a purpose in life and a sense of direction.

-J. Martin Klotsche

I conceive that pleasures are to be avoided if greater pains be the consequence, and pains to be coveted that will terminate in greater pleasures.

-Anonymous

Many receive advice. Only the wise profit by it.

-Publilius Syrus

The secret of success of every man who has ever been successful lies in the fact that he formed the habit of doing those things that failures don't like to do.

-A. Jackson King

Quality is never an accident; it is always the result of high intention, sincere effort, intelligent direction and skillful execution; it represents the wise choice of many alternatives.

-Anonymous

It is the paradox of life that the way to miss pleasure is to seek it first. The very first condition of lasting happiness is that a life should be full of purpose, aiming at something outside one's self. As a matter of experience, we find that true happiness comes in seeking other things in the manifold activities of life, in the healthful outgoing of all human powers.

-Hugo Black

Wisdom is to the mind what health is to the body.

-Francois La Rochefoucauld

Hold yourself responsible for a higher standard than anybody else expects of you.

-Anonymous

Thoughts lead on to purposes; purposes go forth in action; actions form habits; habits decide character; and character fixes our destiny.

-Tyron Edwards

We are what we think. All that we are arises with our thoughts. With our thoughts, we make our world.

-Anonymous

Life is divided into three terms: that which was, which is and which will be. Let us learn from the past to profit by the present and, from the present to live better for the future.

-William Wordsworth

The measure of a man's real character is what he would do if he knew he would never be found out.

-MacAulay

Live life fully while you are here. Experience everything. Take care of yourself and your friends. Have fun. Let your humanity, your caring for yourself and others be the guiding principle of your life, but don't treat life so seriously that you lose the power of spontaneity, the pleasure that comes from being silly and being a kid.

-Anonymous

Wisdom is knowing when to speak your mind and when to mind your speech.

-Evangel

All things come to him who waits, provided he knows what he is waiting for.

-Woodrow Wilson

Nothing in life is to be feared. It is only to be understood.

-Marie Curie

One should count each day a separate life.

-Seneca

Nothing splendid has ever been achieved except by those who dared believe that something inside of them was superior to circumstance.

-Anonymous

Fear is an insidious virus. Given a breeding place in our minds, it will permeate the whole body of our work. It will eat away our spirit and block the forward path of our endeavors. Fear is the greatest enemy of progress. Progress moves ever on and does not linger to consider microscopically the implications of each particular action. Only small and overcautious minds see the shadows of lurking enemies and dangers everywhere and shrink away from the increased efforts needed to overcome them. Fear is met and destroyed with courage. Again and again, when the struggle seems hopeless and all opportunity lost, some man or woman with a little more courage, a little more effort, brings victory.

-James F. Bell

In the middle of difficulty lies opportunity.

-Anonymous

Experience is not what happens to a man. It is what a man does with what happens to him.

-Aldous Huxley

For anything worth having, one must pay the price: and the price is always work, patience, love, self sacrifice; no paper currency, no promises to pay, but the gold of real service.

-John Burroughs

If we are ever to enjoy life, now is the time, not tomorrow, nor next year, nor in some future life after we have died. The best preparation for a better life next year is a full, complete, harmonious, joyous life this year. Our beliefs in a rich future life are of little importance unless we coin them into rich present life. Today should always be our most wonderful day.

-Thomas Dreier

Use what talents you possess. The woods would be very silent if no birds sang there except those that sang best.

-Anonymous

The best time to frame an answer to the letters of a friend is the moment you receive them; then the warmth of friendship and the intelligence received most forcibly cooperate.

-William Sprague

The quality of a person's life is in direct proportion to their commitment to excellence.

-Anonymous

The man who lives for himself is a failure. Even if he gains much wealth, position or power, he still is a failure. The man who lives for others has achieved true success. A rich man who consecrates his wealth and his position to the good of humanity is a success. A poor man who gives of his service and his sympathy to others has achieved true success even though material prosperity or outward honors never come to him.

-Norman Vincent Peale, D.D.

Today a reader, tomorrow a leader.

-W. Fusselman

There are defining moments in a life, when faced with the choice of giving up or going on.

-Anonymous

The only time you don't want to fail is the last time you try.

-Charles F. Kettering

Of all the blessings that time and earth bestow, there is none so precious as one true friend.

-Anonymous

What makes greatness is starting something that lives after you.

-Ralph W. Sockman

No man has a good enough memory to be a successful liar.

-Abraham Lincoln

There is no exercise better for the heart than reaching down and lifting people up.

-John Andrew Holmes

Happiness is a hard thing because it is achieved only by making others happy.

-Stuart Cloete

The superior man thinks always of virtue; the common man thinks of comfort.

-Confucius

The difference between a successful person and others is not a lack of strength, not a lack of knowledge, but rather in a lack of will.

-Anonymous

The happy people are those who are producing something; the bored people are those who are consuming much and producing nothing.

-William Ralph Inge

There is little peace or comfort in life if we are always anxious as to future events. He that worries himself with the dread of possible contingencies will never be at rest.

-Samuel Johnson

If we command our wealth, we shall be rich and free. If our wealth commands us, we are poor indeed.

-Edmund Burke

The race is not always to the swift, but to those who keep on running.

-Anonymous

One who fears failure limits his activities. Failure is the only opportunity to intelligently begin again.

-Henry Ford

If your business keeps you so busy that you have no time for anything else, there must be something wrong, either with you or with your business.

-William J.H. Boetcker

Silence is one great art of conversation. He is not a fool who knows when to hold his tongue; and a person may gain credit for sense, eloquence, wit, who merely says nothing to lessen the opinion which others have of these qualities in themselves.

-William Hazlitt

Live for today. Multitudes of people have failed to live for today. They have spent their lives reaching for the future. What they have had within their grasp today, they have missed entirely because only the future has intrigued them and the first thing they knew, the future became the past; too late had they come to that realization, and when finally it dawned upon them, they realized that life upon this earth was very fleeting and they realized the truth of the observation that
*A thousand years are as but a day.*

-William Allen White

Money and time are the heaviest burdens of life, and the unhappiest of all mortals are those who have more of either than they know how to use.

-Samuel Johnson

Do not follow where the path may lead. Go instead where there is no path and leave a trail.

-Anonymous

The only security is courage.

-Francois La Rochefoucauld

Obstacles are those frightful things you see when you take your eyes off the goal.

-Hannah More

You cannot discover new oceans unless you have the courage to lose sight of the shore.

-Anonymous

Men spend their lives in anticipation, in determining to be vastly happy at some period when they have time. But, the present time has one advantage over every other, it is our own. Past, the opportunities are gone, future are not come. We may lay in a stock of pleasures as we would lay in a stock of wine; but, if we defer the tasting of them too long, we shall find that both are soured by age.

-Colton

I have learned that success is to be measured not so much by the position that one has reached in life as by the obstacles which he has overcome while trying to succeed.

-Booker T. Washington

Life affords no higher pleasure than that of surmounting difficulties, passing from one step of success to another, forming new wishes and seeing them gratified. He that labors in any great or laudable undertaking has his fatigues first supported by hope and afterwards rewarded by joy.
-Samuel Johnson

Children are always the only future the human race has. Teach them well.
-Anonymous

Think, listen and read for ideas. Don't be afraid to speak up freely and fully about your ideas. Be ready to give and take criticism on ideas. Share your knowledge with others and be willing to take a share of their ideas if they are good. Keep an open mind until you have learned as much as possible and then evaluate and make your decision.
-Arthur Eisenstadt

We need fewer philosophies and more philosophers.
-Frank Romer

When the day is over and you have done your best, wait the results in peace.

-Anonymous

The way of a superior man is threefold. Virtuous, he is free from anxieties; wise, he is free from perplexities; bold, he is free from fear.

-Confucius

Sometimes we may learn more from a man's errors than from his virtues.

-Henry Wadsworth Longfellow

Research means that you don't know, but are willing to find out.

-Charles F. Kettering

Every job is a self portrait of the person who did it. Autograph your work with excellence.

-Anonymous

A good scare is worth more to a man than advice.

-Edgar Watson Howe

There are dreamers and there are planners; the planners make their dreams come true.

-Anonymous

When nothing seems to help, I go and look at a stonecutter hammering away at his rock, perhaps a hundred times without as much as a crack showing in it. Yet, at the hundred and first blow it will split in two and I know it was not that last blow that did it, but all that had gone before.

-Jacob A. Riis

If you want to earn more, learn more. If you want to get more out of the world, you must put more into the world. For, after all, men will get no more out of life than they put into it.

-William J.H. Boetcker

Keep on going and the chances are that you will stumble on something, perhaps when you are least expecting it. I have never heard of anyone stumbling on something sitting down.

-Charles F. Kettering

Money dishonestly acquired is never worth its cost, while a good conscience never costs as much as it is worth.

-J.P. Senn

Nothing is a waste of time if you use the experience wisely.

-Auguste Rodin

A life lived in fear is a life half lived.

-Anonymous

Leisure for men of business and business for men of leisure would cure many complaints.

-Hesther Thrale

It is better to lay your life upon the altar of worthy endeavor than to luxuriate and perish as a weed.

-Albert L. Williams

Success usually comes to those who are too busy to be looking for it.

-Henry David Thoreau

Anyone can hold the helm when the sea is calm.
-Anonymous

To grow and know what one is growing towards, that is the source of all strength and confidence in life.
-James Baillie

If a man has a talent and cannot use it, he has failed. If he has a talent and uses only half of it, he has partly failed. If he has a talent and learns somehow to use the whole of it, he has gloriously succeeded and won a satisfaction and a triumph few men will ever know.
-Thomas Wolfe

The block of granite which was an obstacle in the path of the weak becomes a stepping stone in the path of the strong.
-Thomas Carlyle

Minds are like parachutes; they only function when open.
-Thomas Dewar

Security is mostly a superstition. It does not exist in nature, nor do the children of men as a whole experience it. Avoiding danger is no safer in the long run than outright exposure. The fearful are caught as often as the bold. Faith alone defends.

-Helen Keller

The only failure which lacks dignity is the failure to try.

-Malcolm F. MacNeil

The difference between one man and another is not mere ability, it is energy.

-Thomas Arnold

*Carpe Diem* - Seize the day: The enjoyment of pleasures of the moment without concern for the future.

-Anonymous

The greatest mistake you can make in life is to be continually fearing you will make one.

-Elbert Hubbard

The fool wanders, the wise man travels.
-Thomas Fuller

Any fool can criticize, condemn and complain, and most fools do.
-Dale Carnegie

You are your greatest investment. The more you store in that mind of yours, the more you enrich your experience, the more people you meet, the more books you read, and the more places you visit, the greater is that investment in all that you are. Everything that you add to your peace of mind and to your outlook upon life is added capital that no one but yourself can dissipate.
-George Matthew Adams

Everyday is a new life to a wise man.
-Anonymous

The greatest test of courage on earth is to bear defeat without losing heart.
-Robert Green Ingersoll

I do the very best I know how, the very best I can, and mean to keep doing so until the end. If the end brings me out all right, what is said against me won't amount to anything. If the end brings me out wrong, ten angels swearing I was right would make no difference.

-Abraham Lincoln

Your fears can be overcome if you deal with them properly. Fear is an emotion. Emotions come wholly from within and have only the strength we allow them. As human beings, we enjoy the possession of an intellect, and it is the intellect, not the emotions, that must be the supreme guiding force of our lives if we are to know any measure of happiness here. Emotions are the color of life; we would be drab creatures indeed without them. But, we must control those emotions or they will control us. This is particularly true of the emotion of fear, which if allowed free rein would reduce all of us to trembling shadows of men for whom only death could bring release.

-John M. Wilson

The road to success is usually off the beaten path.
-Frank Tyger

Know the true value of time; snatch, seize, and enjoy every moment of it. No idleness, no laziness or procrastination.
-Lord Chesterfield

Things may come to those who wait, but only the things left by those who hustle.
-Abraham Lincoln

Face your fears and the death of fear is certain.
-Anonymous

It is better to say, "I don't know," than to lie about it.
-Ignas Bernstein

One never learns by success. Success is the plateau that one rests upon to take a breath and look down from upon the straight and difficult path, but one does not climb upon a plateau.
-Josephine Preston Peabody

Lack of will power and drive cause more failure than lack of imagination and ability.

-Dennis Mahoney

Happy are those who dream dreams and are ready to pay the price to make them come true.

-Leon J. Suenens

Courage is what it takes to stand up and speak; courage is also what it takes to sit down and listen.

-Winston S. Churchill

We are what we repeatedly do. Excellence, then, is not an act but a habit.

-Anonymous

One of the greatest talents of all is the talent to recognize and to develop talent in others.

-Frank Tyger

Lincoln was not great because he was born in a log cabin, but because he got out of it.

-James Truslow Adams

When you like your work, every day is a holiday.
-Frank Tyger

The most valuable of talents is that of never using two words when one will do.
-Thomas Jefferson

You can make more friends in two months by becoming really interested in other people than you can in two years by trying to get other people interested in you.
-Dale Carnegie

Braving obstacles and hardships is nobler than retreat to tranquillity. The butterfly that hovers around the lamp until it dies is more admirable than the mole that lives in the dark tunnel.
-Kahlil Gibran

Man cannot degrade woman without himself falling into degradation; he cannot elevate her without at the same time elevating himself.
-Alexander Walker

Good people are good because they've come to wisdom through failure.

-William Saroyan

Wisdom is knowing what to do next. Virtue is doing it.

-David Starr Jordan

People don't care how much you know, they want to know how much you care.

-Anonymous

Never close your lips to those to whom you have opened your heart.

-Charles Dickens

When it's time to die, let us not discover that we have never lived.

-Henry David Thoreau

Success comes to those who know it isn't coming to them and who go out to get it.

-Frank Tyger

To laugh often and much; to win the respect of intelligent people and the affection of children; to earn the appreciation of honest critics and endure the betrayal of false friends; to appreciate beauty; to find the best in others; to leave the world a bit better whether by a healthy child, a garden patch, or a redeemed social condition; to know even one life has breathed easier because you lived. This is to have succeeded.

-Ralph Waldo Emerson

He who makes no mistakes never makes anything.

-English Proverb

Many persons have a wrong idea of what constitutes true happiness. It is not attained through self-gratification, but through fidelity to a worthy purpose.

-Helen Keller

The most important thing a father can do for his children is to love their mother.

-Theodore Hesburgh

No time of life is so beautiful as the early days of love, when with every meeting, every glance, one fetches something new to rejoice over.

-Soren Kierkegaard

The longer I live, the more deeply I am convinced that which makes the difference between one man and another, between the weak and the powerful, the great and the insignificant, is energy, invisible determination, a purpose once formed and then death or victory. This quality will do anything that has to be done in the world and no talents, no circumstances, no opportunities, will make one a man without it.

-Thomas Buxton

Plan ahead: It wasn't raining when Noah built the ark.

-Richard Cushing

Our true acquisitions lie only in our charities. We get only as we give.

-William Simms

To love praise, but not worship it, and fear condemnation, but not go down under it, is evidence of a well-balanced personality.

-Anonymous

When one door is shut, another opens.

-Miguel de Cervantes

Happiness is someone to love, something to do, and something to hope for.

-Chinese Proverb

He who walks in another's tracks leaves no footprints.

-Joan L. Brannon

Worry is interest paid on trouble before it becomes due.

-William Ralph Inge

Tact is the knack of making a point without making an enemy.

-Howard W. Newton

Never doubt that a small group of thoughtful, committed people can change the world. Indeed, it is the only thing that ever has.

-Anonymous

The successful man lengthens his stride when he discovers that the signpost has deceived him; the failure looks for a place to sit down.

-J.R. Rogers

Life is either a daring adventure or nothing.

-Helen Keller

To live without loving is not really to live.

-Moliere

An optimist sees an opportunity in every calamity; a pessimist sees a calamity in every opportunity.

-Winston S. Churchill

The greatest misfortune of all is not to be able to bear misfortune.

-Bias

Fear is the main source of superstition and one of the main sources of cruelty. To conquer fear is the beginning of wisdom.

-Bertrand Russell

You are the product of your heredity, environment, physical body, conscious and subconscious mind, experience and particular position and direction in time and space. You have the powers to affect, use, control or harmonize with all of them. You can direct your thoughts, control your emotions and ordain your destiny.

-Anonymous

Success is a journey, not a destination.

-H. Tom Collard

In seeking honey, expect the sting of bees.

-Arabian Proverb

You never get a second chance to make a good first impression.

-Will Rogers

Try leaving a friendly trail of little sparks of gratitude on your daily trips. You will be surprised how they set small fires that will be rose beacons on your next visit.

-Anonymous

There isn't much thrill in success unless one has first been close to failure.

-William Feather

Nothing is so contagious as enthusiasm.

-Edward George Bulwer-Lytton

A pint of sweat will save a gallon of blood.

-George S. Patton

Some men see things as they are and ask, *"Why?"* I dream things that never were and ask, *"Why not?"*

-Robert F. Kennedy

Happiness is not a station you arrive at, but a manner of traveling.

-Margaret Lee Runbeck

Fortunate people often have favorable beginnings and very tragic endings. What matters isn't being applauded when you arrive, for that is common, but being missed when you leave.

-Baltasar Gracian

Do not be too timid and squeamish about your actions. All life is an experiment.

-Ralph Waldo Emerson

We climb to heaven mostly on the ruins of our cherished plans, finding that our failures were but friendly guide posts that led us onward and upward toward success.

-Anonymous

A ship in harbor is safe, but that is not what ships are built for.

-John Shedd

The optimist says we live in the best of all possible worlds; the pessimist fears this is true.

-James Branch Cabell

For success, attitude is equally as important as ability.
-Harry F. Banks

That man is richest whose pleasures are the cheapest.
-Henry David Thoreau

Education is that which remains when one has forgotten everything he learned in school.
-Albert Einstein

Success is getting what you want; happiness is wanting what you get.
-Dave Gardner

If you find a path with no obstacles, it probably doesn't lead anywhere.
-Frank A. Clark

If you must slander someone, don't speak it. Write it in sand near the waters edge.
-Anonymous

If you want a place in the sun, you must leave the shade of the family tree.

-Osage Saying

He conquers who endures.

-Italian Proverb

The only man who is really free is the one who can turn down an invitation to dinner without giving an excuse.

-Jules Renard

Ask any wise man what he so desires and he will answer, more wisdom.

-Anonymous

Fear not for the future; weep not for the past.

-Percy Bysshe Shelley

When one door closes another door opens; but we often look so long and so regretfully upon the closed door that we do not see the ones which open for us.

-Alexander Graham Bell

Progress is not created by contented people.
-Frank Tyger

Don't ask the barber whether you need a haircut.
-Daniel S. Greenberg

Don't go around saying the world owes you a living; the world owes you nothing, it was here first.
-Mark Twain

Far better it is to dare mighty things, to win glorious triumphs even though checkered by failure, than to rank with those poor spirits who neither enjoy nor suffer much because they live in the gray twilight that knows neither victory nor defeat.
-Theodore Roosevelt

Many of life's failures are people who did not realize how close they were to success when they gave up.
-Thomas A. Edison

Fall seven times, stand up eight.
-Japanese Proverb

Life moves on whether we act as cowards or heroes. Life has no other discipline to impose, if we would but realize it, than to accept life unquestioningly. Everything we shut our eyes to, everything we run away from, everything we deny, denigrate or despise, serves to defeat us in the end. What seems nasty, painful, evil, can become a source of beauty, joy and strength, if faced with an open mind. Every moment is a golden one for him who has the vision to recognize it as such.

-Henry Miller

If you have tried and met with defeat; if you have planned and watched your plans as they were crushed before your eyes; just remember that the greatest men in all history were the products of courage, and courage, you know, is born in the cradle of adversity.

-Anonymous

A man must so train his habits as to rely upon his courage in moments of emergency.

-Orison Swett Marden

Procrastination is the fear of success. People procrastinate because they are afraid of the success that they know will result if they move ahead now. Because success is heavy, carries a responsibility with it, it is much easier to procrastinate and live on the "someday I'll" philosophy.

-Denis Waitley

Pessimism leads to weakness; optimism to power.

-William James

If you love something so much, set it free; if it never comes back, it was never meant to be; if it returns to you, its yours forever.

-Anonymous

Success is not the result of spontaneous combustion. You must set yourself on fire.

-Reggie Leach

Never allow your energy or enthusiasm to be dampened by the discouragements that inevitably come.

-James Whitcomb Riley

There are eight requisites for contented living: health enough to make work a pleasure; wealth enough to support your needs; strength to battle with difficulties and overcome them; grace enough to confess your sins and forsake them; patience enough to toil until some good is accomplished; charity enough to see some good in your neighbor; faith enough to make real the things of God; hope enough to remove all anxious fear concerning the future.

-Goethe

A miracle is often the willingness to see the common in an uncommon way; strength is not the absence of weakness, but how we wrestle with our weaknesses.

-Howard Schultz

The power of an idea can be measured by the degree of resistance it attracts.

-David Yoho

Happiness is not having what you want; it is wanting what you have.

-Anonymous

The real secret of success is enthusiasm.
-Walter Chrysler

The Lord gave us two ends, one to sit on and one to think with. Success depends on which one we use the most.
-Ann Landers

My grandfather once told me that there are two kinds of people: those who do the work and those who take the credit. He told me to try to be in the first group, there was less competition there.
-Indira Gandhi

Be more concerned with your character than your reputation, because your character is what you really are, while your reputation is merely what others think you are.
-Anonymous

He who never made a mistake never made a discovery.
-Samuel Smiles

He who never failed somewhere, that man can not be great.

-Herman Melville

God gives every bird its food, but He does not throw it into the nest.

-J.G. Holland

Persistence is what makes the impossible, *possible*; the possible, *likely;* and the likely, *definite.*

-Robert Half

Life is not a goblet to be drained. It is a measure to be filled.

-Anonymous

You may have to fight a battle more than once to win it.

-Margaret Thatcher

Don't part with your illusions. When they are gone, you may still exist, but you have ceased to live.

-Mark Twain

No mistakes, no experience, no wisdom.
-Stanley Goldstein

The measure of a man is the way he bears up under misfortune.
-Plutarch

Some people make things happen, some watch things happen, while others wonder what has happened.
-Anonymous

Acceptance of what has happened is the first step to overcoming the consequences of any misfortune.
-William James

Courage is resistance to fear, mastery of fear, not absence of fear.
-Mark Twain

Great works are performed not by strength, but by perseverance.
-Samuel Johnson

If I had my life to live over again, I would dare to make more mistakes next time. I would relax. I would limber up. I would be sillier than I have been this trip. I would take fewer things seriously. I would take more chances. I would take more trips. I would climb more mountains and swim more rivers. I would eat more ice cream and less beans. I would, perhaps, have more actual troubles, but fewer imaginary ones. You see, I am one of those people who was sensible and sane, hour after hour, day after day. Oh, I have had my moments. If I had it to do over again, I would have more of them. In fact, I would try to have nothing else, just moments, one after another, instead of living so many years ahead of each day. I have been one of those persons who never goes anywhere without a thermometer, a hot water bottle, a raincoat and a parachute. If I could do it again, I would travel lighter than I have. If I had my life to live over, I would start barefoot earlier in the spring and stay that way later in the fall. I would go to more dances. I would ride more merry-go-rounds. I would pick more daisies.

-Nadine Stair

Cherish your visions and your dreams as they are the children of your soul; the blueprint of your ultimate achievements.

-Anonymous

Effort fully releases its reward only after a person refuses to quit.

-Napoleon Hill

The harder you work, the harder it is to surrender.

-Vincent T. Lombardi

You become a champion by fighting one more round.

-James T. Corbett

The beauty of the soul shines out when a man bears with composure one heavy mischance after another; not because he does not feel them, but because he is a man of high and heroic temper.

-Aristotle

Never give up; never, never, never, never give up.

-Winston S. Churchill

Giving people a little more than they expect is a good way to get back a lot more than you'd expect.

-Robert Half

Winner vs. Loser. The winner is always part of the answer. The loser is always part of the problem. The winner always has a program. The loser always has an excuse. The winner says, "Let me do it for you." The loser says, "That's not my job." The winner sees an answer for every problem. The loser sees a problem for every answer. The winner sees a green near every sand trap. The loser sees two or three sand traps near every green. The winner says, "It may be difficult but it's possible." The loser says, "It may be possible, but it's too difficult." Be a winner.

-Anonymous

The social fabric of a well-established nation is tough stuff. It can be pulled around and stretched a considerable distance before it breaks. But, when the final rupture comes, the damage done is by repair.

-H.W. Prentis, Jr.

It is the mind that maketh good of ill, that maketh wretch or happy, rich or poor.

-Edmund Spenser

Control your destiny or someone else will.

-Anonymous

Your chances of success in any undertaking can always be measured by your belief in yourself.

-Robert Collier

The high prize of life, the crowning glory of a man, is to be born with a bias to some pursuit which finds him in employment and happiness; whether it be to make baskets, or broadswords, or canals, or statues, or songs.

-Ralph Waldo Emerson

There is little difference in people, but that little difference makes a big difference. The little difference is attitude. The big difference is whether it is positive or negative.

-W. Clement Stone

Success seems to be largely a matter of hanging on after others have let go.

-William Feather

If you're feeling low, don't despair. The sun has a sinking spell every night, but it comes up every morning.

-Anonymous

It is right and proper to support rigorously our way of living as being the greatest in the world, but it is not right and proper to be blind to its weakness.

-John F. Kennedy

Little minds are tamed and subdued by misfortunes; but great minds rise above them.

-Washington Irving

If things are not going well with you, begin your effort at correcting the situation by carefully examining the service you are rendering, and especially the spirit in which you are rendering it.

-Roger Babson

Welcome ever more to gods and men is the self-helping man.

-Ralph Waldo Emerson

Although wealth may not bring happiness, the immediate prospect of it provides a wonderfully close imitation.

-Patrick O'Brian

You can live without loving, but you can't love without giving.

-Michael Douglas

Far away, there in the sunshine, are my highest aspirations. I may not reach them, but I can look up and see their beauty, believe in them and try to follow where they lead.

-Anonymous

Pleasure is nature's test, her sign of approval. When man is happy, he is in harmony with himself and with his environment.

-Oscar Wilde

The good things of prosperity are to be wished; but the good things that belong to adversity are to be admired.

-Seneca

Whatever task you undertake, do it with all your heart and soul. Always be courteous, never be discouraged. Beware of him who promises something for nothing. Do not blame anybody for your mistakes and failures. Do not look for approval except the consciousness of doing your best.

-Bernard M. Baruch

We often pray for purity, unselfishness, for the highest qualities of character, and forget that these things cannot be given, but must be earned.

-Lyman Abbott

If you will call your *troubles, experiences,* and remember that every experience develops some latent force within you, you will grow vigorous and happy however adverse your circumstances may seem to be.

-J.R. Miller

Persistence prevails when all else fails. Opportunity always involves some risk. You can't steal second base and keep your foot on first.

-Anonymous

If you want to succeed, you should strike out on new paths rather than travel the worn paths of accepted success.

-John D. Rockefeller

Nothing happens unless first a dream.

-Carl Sandburg

Enjoyment is not a goal, it is a feeling that accompanies important ongoing activity.

-Paul Goodman

I think luck is the sense to recognize an opportunity and the ability to take advantage of it. Every one has bad breaks, but every one also has opportunities. The man who can smile at his breaks and grab his chances gets on.

-Samuel Goldwyn

The key to happiness is having dreams. The key to success is making dreams come true.

-Anonymous

The great pleasure in life is doing what people say you cannot do.

-Walter Bagehot

Life is like riding a bicycle. You don't fall off unless you stop pedaling.

-Claude Pepper

Do it the hard way! Think ahead of your job. Then, nothing in the world can keep the job ahead from reaching out for you. Do it better than it need be done. Next time doing it will be child's play. Let no one or anything stand between you and the difficult task. Let nothing deny you this rich chance to gain strength by adversity, confidence by mastery, success by deserving it. Do it better each time. Do it better than anyone else can do it. I know this sounds old-fashioned. It is, but it has built the world.

-Harlow H. Curtice

The future belongs to those who believe in the beauty of their dreams.

-Eleanor Roosevelt

The greatest remedy for anger is delay.

-Seneca

Whoever serves his country well has no need of ancestors.

-Francois Marie Arouet Voltaire

Success is the quality of your journey.

-Jennifer James

The gem cannot be polished without friction, nor man perfected without trials.

-Chinese Proverb

He who wishes to fulfill his mission in the world must be a man of one idea, that is, of one great overmastering purpose, overshadowing all his aims, and guiding and controlling his entire life.

-Bate

The big salaries in business always go to those who have what it takes to get things done. That is true not only of those executives who guide the destinies of a business, but it is true of those upon whom those executives must depend for results.

-J.C. Aspley

The loftier your goals, the higher your risk, the greater your glory.

-Anonymous

Nothing can stop the man with the right mental attitude from achieving his goal; nothing on earth can help the man with the wrong mental attitude.

-W.W. Ziege

When you look at the world in a narrow way, how narrow it seems! When you look at it in a mean way, how mean it is! When you look at it selfishly, how selfish it is! But, when you look at it in a broad, generous, friendly spirit, what wonderful people you find in it!

-Horace Rutledge

Life without risk is no life at all.
-Anonymous

Knowledge is the eye of desire and can become the pilot of the soul.
-Will Durant

It is a fine thing to have ability, but the ability to discover the ability in others is the true test.
-Elbert Hubbard

Well done is better than well said.
-Benjamin Franklin

An acre of performance is worth a whole world of promise.
-W.D. Howells

Perfectionism is a dangerous state of mind in an imperfect world. The best way is to forget doubts and set about the task in hand. If you are doing your best, you will not have time to worry about failure.
-Robert Hillyer

Aim at perfection in everything, though in most things it is unattainable. However, they who aim at it, and persevere, will come much nearer to it than those whose laziness and despondency make them give it up as unattainable.

-Lord Chesterfield

Men in general are too material and do not make enough human contacts. If we search for the fundamentals which actually motivate us, we will find that they come under four headings: love, money, adventure and religion. It is to some of them that we always owe that big urge which pushes us onward. Men who crush these impulses and settle down to everyday routine are bound to sink into mediocrity. No man is a complete unit of himself; he needs the contact, the stimulus and the driving power which is generated by his contact with other men, their ideas and constantly changing scenes.

-Edward S. Jordan

The sky's the limit when your heart is in it.

-Anonymous

We cannot always oblige, but we can always speak.
-Francois Marie Arouet Voltaire

The future belongs to those who believe in the beauty of their dreams.
-Anonymous

The simple virtues of willingness, readiness, alertness and courtesy will carry a man farther than mere smartness.
-Davidson

The real gentleman is one who is gentle in everything, at least in everything that depends on himself; in carriage, temper, constructions, aims, desires. He is mild, calm, quiet, even temperate; not hasty in judgment, not exorbitant in ambition, not overbearing, not proud, not rapacious, not oppressive.
-Hare

Talk happiness. The world is sad enough without your woe.
-Orison Swett Marden

All problems become smaller if you don't dodge them, but confront them. Touch a thistle timidly and it pricks you, grasp it boldly and its spines crumble.

-William S. Halsey

To do anything in this world worth doing, we must not stand back shivering and thinking of the cold and danger, but jump in and scramble through as well as we can.

-Sydney Smith

When you make a mistake, don't look back at it too long. Take the reason of the thing into your mind and then look forward. Mistakes are lessons of wisdom. The past cannot be changed. The future is yet in your power.

-Hugh White

If it is to be, it is up to me.

-Anonymous

Reprove thy friend privately; commend him publicly.

-Solon

I love the man that can smile in trouble, that can gather strength from distress and grow brave by reflection. 'Tis the business of little minds to shrink, but he whose heart is firm and whose conscience approves his conduct will pursue his principles unto death.

-Thomas Paine

I keep the telephone of my mind open to peace, harmony, health, love and abundance. Then, whenever doubt, anxiety or fear try to call me, they keep getting a busy signal and they'll soon forget my number.

-Edith Armstrong

Pay as little attention to discouragement as possible. Plough ahead as a steamer does, rough or smooth, rain or shine. To carry your cargo and make your port is the point.

-Maltbie Babcock

Don't wait for your ship to come in. Swim out to it.

-Anonymous

It is never safe to look into the future with eyes of fear.
-Edward H. Harriman

The pleasure you get from your life is equal to the attitude you put into it.
-Anonymous

Fortunate is the person who has developed the self-control to steer a straight course toward his objective in life without being swayed from his purpose by either commendation or condemnation.
-Napoleon Hill

Action may not always bring happiness, but there is no happiness without action.
-Benjamin Disraeli

How to forgive is something we have to learn, not as a duty or an obligation, but as an experience akin to the experience of love; it must come into being spontaneously.
-Theodore Cuyler Speers, D.D.

Goodness is always an asset. A man who is straight, friendly and useful may never be famous, but he is respected and liked by all who know him. He has laid a sound foundation for success and he will have a worth-while life.

-Herbert N. Casson

Don't be a fault-finding grouch. When you feel like finding fault with somebody or something stop for a moment and think. There is very apt to be something wrong within yourself. Don't permit yourself to show temper, and always remember that when you are in the right you can afford to keep your temper, and when you are in the wrong you cannot afford to lose it.

-J.J. Reynolds

Life is too short to be unhappy in business. If business were not a part of the joy of living, we might almost say that we have no right to live, because it is a pretty poor man who cannot get into the line for which he is fitted.

-George L. Brown

There are but two powers in the world, the sword and the mind. In the long run, the sword is always beaten by the mind.

-Napoleon Hill

It takes courage to live; courage and strength and hope and humor. And courage and strength and hope and humor have to be bought and paid for with pain and work and prayers and tears.

-Jerome P. Fleishman

The rung of a ladder was never meant to rest upon, but only to hold a man's foot long enough to enable him to put the other somewhat higher.

-Thomas Henry Huxley

Energy and persistence will conquer all things.

-Anonymous

The trouble with most people is that they think with their hopes or fears or wishes rather than with their minds.

-Walter Duranty

Your morning thoughts may determine your conduct for the day. Optimistic thoughts will make your day bright and productive while pessimistic thinking will make it dull and wasteful. Face each day cheerfully, smilingly and courageously, and it will naturally follow that your work will be a real pleasure and progress will be a delightful accomplishment.

-William M. Peck

Experience shows that success is due less to ability than to zeal. The winner is he who gives himself to his work, body and soul.

-Charles Buxton

We grow great by dreams. All big men are dreamers. They see things in the soft haze of a spring day or in the red fire of a long winter's evening. Some of us let these great dreams die, but others nourish and protect them, nurse them through bad days till they bring them to the sunshine and light which come always to those who sincerely hope that their dreams will come true.

-Woodrow Wilson

Life's greatest achievement is the continual re-making of yourself so that at last you know how to live.

-Winfred Rhodes

They who give, have all things; they who withhold, have nothing.

-Hindu Proverb

We live in the present, we dream of the future and we learn eternal truths from the past.

-Mme. Chiang Kai-shek

Respectable men and women content with the good and easy living are missing some of the most important things in life. Unless you give yourself to some great cause, you haven't even begun to live.

-William P. Merrill, D.D.

Few men during their lifetime come anywhere near exhausting the resources dwelling within them. There are deep wells of strength that are never used.

-Richard E. Byrd

Who hath not known ill fortune, never knew himself or his own virtue.

-Mallette

Either I will find a way or I will make one.

-Sir P. Sidney

If we want more brotherhood and goodwill, more intelligence, more clear thinking, more honesty and sincerity, more tolerance and human understanding, we must concentrate upon cultivating these qualities within ourselves. There is a natural progression in social advancement from the individual spirit to the family, to the community, to the nation and to the world at large. The line of progress can move in no other direction. There is no substitute for personal integrity.

-Howard W. Hintz, D.D.

An aim in life is the only fortune worth finding and it is not to be found in foreign lands, but in the heart itself.

-Anonymous

Do not wallow in the past. You are what you choose today, not what you have chosen in the past.

-Anonymous

On the clarity of your ideas depends the scope of your success in any endeavor.

-James Robertson

No man can tell whether he is rich or poor by turning to his ledger. It is the heart that makes a man rich. He is rich according to what he is, not according to what he has.

-Henry Ward Beecher

If the average person realized the power he wields over his own life and destiny, he would live in a perpetual state of wonder and thanksgiving.

-Anonymous

Decision is a sharp knife that cuts clean and straight; indecision, a dull one that hacks and tears and leaves ragged edges behind it.

-Gordon Graham

No matter how much madder it may make you, get out of bed forcing a smile. You may not smile because you are cheerful; but if you will force yourself to smile, you'll end up laughing. You will be cheerful because you smile. Repeated experiments prove that when man assumes the facial expression of a given mental mood, any given mood, then that mental mood itself will follow.

-Kenneth Goode

The sole meaning of life is to serve humanity.

-Tolstoi

Life is like a grindstone: Whether it grinds you down or polishes you up depends on what you're made of.

-Anonymous

The most difficult thing in life is to know yourself.

-Thales

A prudent person profits from personal experience, a wise one from the experience of others.

-Dr. Joseph Collins

When you talk about your troubles, your ailments, your diseases, your hurts, you give longer life to what makes you unhappy. Talking about your grievances merely adds to those grievances. Give recognition only to what you desire. Think and talk only about the good things that add to your enjoyment of your work and life. If you don't talk about your grievances, you'll be delighted to find them disappearing quickly.

-Thomas Dreier

Fear is an acid which is pumped into one's atmosphere. It causes mental, moral and spiritual asphyxiation and sometimes death; death to energy and all growth.

-Horace Fletcher

Life does not require us to be the biggest or the best, it asks only that we try.

-Anonymous

Waste no tears over the grieves of yesterday.

-Euripides

*I can't do it* never yet accomplished anything; *I will try* has performed wonders.

-George P. Burnham

The only way in which one human being can properly attempt to influence another is by encouraging him to think for himself, instead of endeavoring to instill ready-made opinions into this head.

-Leslie Stephen

You can get anything you want in life if you'll just help enough other people get what they want.

-Anonymous

Chance favors the prepared mind.

-Louis Pasteur

Mere enrollment will not make one a scholar; the pupil must continue in the school through the long course until he masters every branch. Success depends upon staying power. The reason for failure in most cases is lack of perseverance.

-J.R. Miller

Anyone who has had a long life of experience is worth listening to, worth emulating and worth tying to as a friend. No one can have too much experience in any line of endeavor. We readily welcome to our group of friends that one who talks with the voice of experience and common sense. We know that we are safe in his hands. He is not going to get us into trouble. Rather is he going to point out the pitfalls and mistakes that experience has taught him to avoid. There is no experience but what carries its lasting good for us along with it. And you don't have to discard experience. It's a coat for life! It never wears out.

-George Matthew Adams

You cannot discover new oceans unless you have the courage to lose sight of the shore.

-Anonymous

We gain nothing by being with such as ourselves; we encourage each other in mediocrity. I am always longing to be with men more excellent than myself.

-Charles Lamb

Good and bad luck is a synonym, in the great majority of instances, for good and bad judgment.

-John Chatfield

Any fool can waste, any fool can muddle, but it takes something of a man to save, and the more he saves, the more of a man does it make of him.

-Rudyard Kipling

The worst bankrupt in the world is the man who has lost his enthusiasm. Let a man lose everything else in the world but his enthusiasm and he will come through again to success.

-H.W. Arnold

The man who actually knows what he wants in life has already gone a long way towards attaining it.

-Anonymous

Worry is a thin stream of fear trickling through the mind. If encouraged, it cuts a channel into which all other thoughts are drained.

-Arthur Somers Roche

Be a life long or short, its completeness depends on what it was lived for.

-David Starr Jordan

The most distinctive mark of a cultured mind is the ability to take another's point of view; to put one's self in another's place and see life and its problems from a point of view different from one's own. To be willing to test a new idea; to be able to live on the edge of difference in all matters intellectually; to examine without hate, the burning question of the day; to have imaginative sympathy, openness and flexibility of mind, steadiness and poise of feeling, cool calmness of judgment, is to have culture.

-A.H.R. Fairchild

No one can predict to what heights you can soar. Even you will not know until you spread your wings.

-Anonymous

I am a great believer in *luck* The harder I work, the more of it I seem to have.

-Coleman Cox

When you approach a problem, strip yourself of preconceived opinions and prejudice, assemble and learn the facts of the situation, make the decision which seems to you to be the most honest, and then stick to it.

-Chester Bowles

It is not strange that we fear most that which never happens. That we destroy our initiative by the fear of defeat, when in reality, defeat is a most useful tonic and should be accepted as such.

-Anonymous

It is not enough to begin; continuance is necessary. Life is a glass given to us to fill; a busy life is filling it with as much as it can hold; a hurried life has had more poured into it than it can contain.

-William Adams Brown

One principle reason why men are so often useless is that they divide and shift their attention among a multiplicity of objects and pursuits.

-Emmons

Agreement makes us soft and complacent; disagreement brings out our strength. Our real enemies are the people who make us feel so good that we are slowly, but inexorably, pulled down into the quicksand of smugness and self-satisfaction.

-Sydney J. Harris

For every action there is an equal and opposite reaction. If you want to receive a great deal, you first have to give a great deal. If each individual will give of himself to whomever he can, wherever he can, in any way that he can, in the long run he will be compensated in the exact proportion that he gives.

-R.A. Hayward

Sometimes one pays most for the things one gets for nothing.

-Albert Einstein

We are all salesmen every day of our lives. We are selling our ideas, our plans, our enthusiasms to those with whom we come in contact.

-Charles M. Schwab

Yesterday is but a dream. Tomorrow is only a vision. But, today well lived, makes every yesterday a dream of happiness and every tomorrow a vision of hope. Look well, therefore, to this day.

-Anonymous

Our definition of success is unorthodox. We claim that any man who is honest, fair, tolerant, kindly, charitable of others and well behaved is a success, no matter what his station in life.

-Jay E. House

Turn obstacles into opportunities and opportunities in profits.

-Anonymous

Whoever in trouble and sorrow needs your help, give it to him. Whoever in anxiety or fear needs your friendship, give it to him. It isn't important whether he likes you. It isn't important whether you approve of his conduct. It isn't important what his creed or nationality may be.

-E.N. West, D.D.

It is better to give love. Hatred is a low and degrading emotion and is so poisonous that no man is strong enough to use it safely. The hatred we think we are directing against some person or thing or system has a devilish way of turning back upon us. When we seek revenge, we administer slow poison to ourselves. When we administer affection, it is astonishing what magical results we obtain.

-Thomas Dreier

There are two things to aim at in life: first, to get what you want; and, after that, to enjoy it. Only the wisest of mankind achieve the second.

-Logan Pearsall Smith

You have failed many times? How fortunate! You ought to know by now, some of the things not to do.

-Anonymous

Humility leads to strength and not to weakness. It is the highest form of self-respect to admit mistakes and to make amends for them.

-John J. McCloy

The superior man is the providence of the inferior. He is eyes for the blind, strength for the weak, and a shield for the defenseless. He stands erect by bending above the fallen. He rises by lifting others.

-Robert Green Ingersoll

Undertake something that is difficult; it will do you good. Unless you try to do something beyond what you have already mastered, you will never grow.

-Ronald E. Osborn

Men must try and try again. They must suffer the consequences of their own mistakes and learn by their own failures and their own successes.

-Lawson Purdy

When a man has put a limit on what he will do, he has put a limit on what he can do.

-Charles M. Schwab

Leaders are like eagles, they don't flock, you find them one at a time.

-Anonymous

Men who have attained things worth having in this world have worked while others idled, have persevered when others gave up in despair, have practiced early in life the valuable habits of self-denial, industry and singleness of purpose. As a result, they enjoyed in later life the success so often erroneously attributed to good luck.

-Grenville Kleiser

Our destiny changes with our thoughts; we shall become what we wish to become, do what we wish to do when our habitual thought corresponds with our desire.

-Orison Swett Marden

When a man begins to understand himself, he begins to live. When he begins to live, he begins to understand his fellow man.

-Norvin G. McGranahan

You never will be the person you can be if pressure, tension and discipline are taken out of your life.

-Dr. James G. Bilkey

The price of wisdom is eternal thought.
-Frank Birch

A man too busy to take care of his health is like a mechanic too busy to take care of his tools.
-Spanish Proverb

A champion is someone who gets up even when they can't.
-Anonymous

Character is power; it makes friends, draws patronage and support and opens a sure way to wealth, honor and happiness.
-J. Howe

Those who command themselves command others.
-William Hazlitt

Man is, properly speaking, based upon hope; he has no other possession but hope; this world of his is emphtically the place of hope.
-Thomas Carlyle

We make a living by what we get. We make a life by what we give.

-Anonymous

No clear-thinking or clear-seeing man or woman can be an apostle of despair. He alone fails who gives up and lies down. To get up each morning with the resolve to be happy; to take anew this attitude of mind whenever the dark or doleful thought presents itself, or whenever the bogeyman stalks into our room or across our path, is to set our own conditions to the events of each day. To do this is to condition circumstances instead of being conditioned by them.

-Ralph Waldo Trine

That man is prudent who neither hopes nor fears anything from the uncertain events of the future.

-Anatole France

Happiness is not so much in having or sharing. We make a living by what we get, but we make a life by what we give.

-Norman MacEwan

A mind, once stretched by a new idea, never regains its original dimension.

-Anonymous

Honesty isn't any policy at all; it's a state of mind or it isn't honesty.

-Eugene L'hote

All men seek one goal: *success* or *happiness.* The only way to achieve true success is to express yourself completely in service to society. First, have a definite, clear, practical ideal: a goal, an objective. Second, have the necessary means to achieve your ends: wisdom, money, materials and methods. Third, adjust all your means to that end.

-Aristotle

Purpose is what gives life a meaning.

-C. H. Parkhurst, D.D.

Habit is either the best of servants or the worst of masters.

-Anonymous

In making a living today, many no longer leave room for life.

-Joseph Sizoo, D.D.

Be not afraid of life. Believe that life is worth living, and your belief will help create the fact.

-William James

I would rather begin at the bottom and climb to the top than to start at the top and have to remain there.

-Anonymous

Our life is what our thoughts make it. A man will find that as he alters his thoughts toward things and other people, things and other people will alter towards him.

-James L. Allen

When an archer misses the mark, he turns and looks for the fault within himself. Failure to hit the bull's-eye is never the fault of the target. To improve your aim, improve yourself.

-Gilbert Arland

Sure! Heart's Desire will come true some day. But you must trust and, trusting, you must wait. You've but to vision to clear the brighter way and see what isn't written on the slate. You must believe that happier, bigger things are coming toward you through the trying year. Your ears must hear the rustle of the wings of God's glad messengers. So, dry your tears! Our trials are tests; our sorrows pave the way for fuller life when we have earned it so. Give rein to faith and hail the brighter day and you shall come, at last, real joy to know.

-Jerome P. Fleishman

To live is not to learn, but to apply.

-Legouve

Without challenge there is no achievement.

-Anonymous

Above all other things is justice. Success is a good thing. Wealth is good, also. Honor is better. But justice exceeds them all.

-David Dudley Field

Great minds have purposes, others have wishes.
-Washington Irving

When dealing with people, remember you are not dealing with creatures of logic, but with creatures of emotion, creatures bristling with prejudice and motivated by pride and vanity.
-Dale Carnegie

Nothing is really work unless you would rather be doing something else.
-Chub De Wolfe

Thought, not money, is the real business capital and, if you know absolutely that what you are doing is right, then you are bound to accomplish it in due season.
-Harvey S. Firestone

Years and years of happiness only make us realize how lucky we are to have friends that have shared and made happiness a reality.
-Robert E. Frederick

A man who suffers before it is necessary, suffers more than is necessary.

-Anonymous

The best way to keep good acts in memory is to refresh them with new.

-Cato

Recipe for success: be polite, prepare yourself for whatever you are asked to do, keep yourself tidy, be cheerful, don't be envious, be honest with yourself so you will be honest with others, be helpful, interest yourself in your job, don't pity yourself, be quick to praise, be loyal to your friends, avoid prejudices, be independent, interest yourself in politics and read the newspapers.

-Bernard M. Baruch

The secret of a good memory is attention, and attention to a subject depends upon our interest in it. We rarely forget that which has made a deep impression on our minds.

-Tyron Edwards

The way to get ahead is to start now. If you start now, you will know a lot next year that you don't know now and that you would not have known next year if you had waited.

-William Feather

The difference between ordinary and extraordinary is the little extra.

-Anonymous

Every failure will teach you a lesson that you need to learn if you will keep your eyes and ears open and be willing to be taught. Every adversity is usually a blessing in disguise. Without reverses and temporary defeat, you would never know the sort of metal of which you are made.

-Napoleon Hill

Time is: Too slow for those who Wait; Too swift for those who Fear; Too long for those who Grieve; Too short for those who Rejoice; but for those who Love, Time is Eternity.

-Henry Van Dyke

Time is a master worker that heals the wounds of temporary defeat.

-Anonymous

Of all the forces that make for a better world, none is so indispensable, none so powerful, as hope. Without hope, men are only half alive. With hope, they dream and think and work.

-Charles Sawyer

If we are to achieve a victorious standard of living today, we must look for the opportunity in every difficulty instead of being paralyzed at the thought of the difficulty in every opportunity.

-Walter E. Cole

An intelligent plan is the first step to success. The man who plans knows where he is going, knows what progress he is making and has a pretty good idea when he will arrive. Planning is the open road to your destination. If you don't know where you are going, how can you expect to get there?

-Basil S. Walsh

You become successful the moment you start moving toward a worthwhile goal.

-Anonymous

To profit from good advice requires more wisdom than to give it.

-Churton Collins

You all have powers you never dreamed of. You can do things you never thought you could do. There are no limitations in what you can do except the limitations in your own mind as to what you cannot do. Don't think you cannot. Think you can.

-Darwin P. Kingsley

Win hearts and you have all men's hands and purses.

-Burleigh

We love peace, but not peace at any price. There is a peace more destructive of the manhood of living man than war is destructive of his body. Chains are worse than bayonets.

-Jerrold

Practice in life whatever you pray for and God will give it to you more abundantly.

-Pusey

People do business with people they like.

-Anonymous

Regret for time wasted can become a power for good in the time that remains.

-Arthur Brisbane

It is a psychological law that whatever we desire to accomplish we must impress upon the subjective or subconscious mind; that is, we must register a vow with ourselves; we must make our resolution with vigor; with faith that we can do the thing we want to do; we must register our conviction with such intensity that the great creative forces within us will tend to realize them. Our impressions will become expressions just inproportion to the vigor with which we register our vows to accomplish our ambitions, to make our visions realities.

-Orison Swett Marden

A trifling kindness here and there is but a simple small affair; yet if your life has sown this free, wide shall your happy harvest be.

-Anonymous

Our business in life is not to get ahead of others, but to get ahead of ourselves, to break our own records, to outstrip our yesterday by our today, to do our work with more force than ever before.

-Stewart B. Johnson

*Know thyself* means this; that you get acquainted with what you know and what you can do.

-Menander

The ability to form friendships, to make people believe in you and trust you is one of the few absolutely fundamental qualities of success. Selling, buying, negotiating are so much smoother and easier when the parties enjoy each other's confidence. The young man who can make friends quickly will find that he will glide instead of stumble through life.

-John J. McGuirk

To me, super salesmanship is not high pressure. It's living 24 hours a day the work you are in, and naturally, extends to every one you contact.

-Otto N. Hahn

To be a winner, all you need to give is all you have.

-Anonymous

The saying that knowledge is power is not quite true. Used knowledge is power. And more than power, it is money, and service, and better living for our fellowmen, and a hundred other good things. But, mere knowledge left unused has not power in it.

-Dr. Edward E. Free

Sometimes the best gain is to lose.

-Lord Herbert

The great gift of conversation lies less in displaying it ourselves than in drawing it out of others. He who leaves your company pleased with himself and his own cleverness is perfectly well pleased with you.

-Jean De La Bruyere

Some succeed because they are destined to. Most succeed because they are determined to.

-Anonymous

He was wise who said, "As I grow older I pay less attention to what men say. I just watch what they do."

-Wilfred A. Peterson

He that never changes his opinions, never corrects his mistakes, will never be wiser on the morrow than he is today.

-Tryon Edwards

We win justice quickest by rendering justice to the other party.

-Mohandas K. Gandhi

It is our individual performances, no matter how humble our place in life may be, that will in the long run determine how well ordered the world may become.

-Paul C. Packer

The foundation of good human relations is friendliness and good will. The right conception of business, in my judgment, is a transaction or a series of transactions carried out in the spirit of friendliness. There are, I know, some people in all walks of life who are so cold-blooded in their attitude that dealings with them chill the blood. There is much more to business than the exchange of material values. We can do business, just as we can carry on all other aspects of our lives, in a wholesome and friendly attitude. When we do so, our days become brighter and happier, more meaningful and more worth-while.

-Charles C. Reigner

You cannot dream yourself into a character; you must hammer and forge one for yourself.

-James A. Froude

If you have a great ambition, take as big a step as possible in the direction of fulfilling it. But, if the step is only a tiny one, don't worry if it is the largest one now possible.

-Mildred McAfee

Instead of loving your enemies, treat your friends a little better.

-Edgar Watson Howe

Whatever you do in life, give it your best shot.

-Anonymous

He who foresees calamities, suffers them twice over.

-Beilby Porteous

Rest has cured more people than all the medicine in the world.

-Harold J. Reilly

Goodwill is the mightiest practical force in the universe.

-Talmudic Saying

The longing to get away from it all never was so great as in our present time of tension and trouble. We want something to lift us out of the mess into which much of life seems to have fallen.

-Glenn Stewart

If we have not peace within ourselves, it is in vain to seek it from outward sources.

-Francois La Rochefoucauld

I believe that if you think about disaster, you will get it. Brood about death and you hasten your demise. Think positively and masterfully, with confidence and faith, and life becomes more secure, more fraught with action, richer in achievement and experience.

-Edward Rickenbacker

Have patience. All things are difficult before they become easy.

-Saadi

Congratulate yourself when you reach that degree of wisdom which prompts you to see less of the weaknesses of others and more of your own.

-Anonymous

True wisdom is to know what is best worth knowing and to do what is best worth doing.

-Edward Porter Humphrey

Man can climb to the highest summits, but he cannot dwell there long.

-George Bernard Shaw

They who have read about everything are thought to understand everything too, but it is not always so. Reading furnishes the mind only with materials of knowledge. It is thinking that makes what we read, ours. We are of the ruminating kind and it is notenough to cram ourselves with a great load of collections, we must chew them over again.

-William Ellery Channing

All men's gains are the fruit of venturing.

-Herodotus

Climb high; climb far. Your goal the sky; your aim the star.

-Anonymous

The superior man is slow in his words and earnest in his conduct.

-Confucius

Every day is a little life, and our whole life is but a day repeated. Therefore, live every day as if it would be the last. Those that dare lose a day are dangerously prodigal. Those that dare misspend it are desperate.

-Joseph Hall

If everyone is moving forward together, then the success takes care of itself.

-Anonymous

When you affirm big, believe big and pray big, big things happen.

-Norman Vincent Peale

There are souls in this world which have the gift of finding joy everywhere and of leaving it behind them when they go.

-Frederick W. Faber

Two men working as a team will produce more than three men working as individuals.

-Alexandre Dumas

It should be our purpose in life to see that each of us makes such a contribution as will enable us to say that we, individually and collectively, are a part of the answer to the world problem and not part of the problem itself.

-Andrew Cordier

The ability to block out the unnecessary puts the goal within reach.

-Anonymous

Peace rules the day where reason rules the mind.

-William Wilkie Collins

The superior man makes the difficulty to be overcome his first interest; success comes only later.

-Confucius

There is a wonderful mythical law of nature that the three things we crave most in life; happiness, freedom and peace of mind are always attained by giving them to someone else.

-Peyton Conway March

Action without study is fatal. Study without action is futile.

-Mary Beard

Be grateful for the joy of life. Be glad for the privilege of work. Be thankful for the opportunity to give and serve. Good work is the great character builder, the sweetener of life, the maker of destiny. Let the spirit of your work be right and, whether your task be great or small, you will then have the satisfaction of knowing it is worth while.

-Grenville Kleiser

Success is not a matter of desire, but the product of hard work.

-Jack Barringer

Accept the challenges so that you may feel the exhilaration.

-Anonymous

Goodness is the only investment which never fails.

-Henry David Thoreau

An effort made for the happiness of others lifts us above ourselves.

-Lydia M. Child

Your living is determined not so much by what life brings to you as by the attitude you bring to life; not so much by what happens to you as by the way your mind looks at what happens. Circumstances and situations do color life, but you have been given the mind to choose what the color shall be.

-John Homer Miller

Every noble work is at first impossible.

-Thomas Carlyle

To stay the course, sometimes you have to make waves.

-Anonymous

In the democratic way of life, it is not *the best things in life are free,* but rather, *the best things in life are worth working for!*

-Ruth M. Leverton

We can easily manage if we will only take, each day, the burden appointed for it. But the load will be too heavy for us if we carry yesterday's burden over again today and then add the burden of the morrow to the weight before we are required to bear it.

-John Newton

The future belongs to those who believe in the beauty of their dreams.

-Anonymous

Politeness is better than logic. You can often persuade when you cannot convince.

-Henry Wheeler Shaw

Happiness is not a reward, it is a consequence. Suffering is not a punishment, it is a result.

-Henry L. Doherty

Tolerance is the positive and cordial effort to understand another's beliefs, practices and habits without necessarily sharing or accepting them.

-Joshua L. Liebman

No one is living a right unless he so lives that whomever meets him goes away more confident and joyous for the contact.

-Anonymous

Try as we may, none of us can be free of conflict and woe. Even the greatest men have had to accept disappointments as their daily bread. The art of living lies less in eliminating our troubles than in growing with them. Man and society must grow together. Each individual's efforts to discipline himself must be matched by society's struggle to enforce the rules of law and of justice under the law.

-Bernard M. Baruch

Look not sorrowfully into the past; it comes not back again. Wisely improve the present; it is thine. Go forth to meet the shadowy future without fear and with a manly heart.

-Henry Wadsworth Longfellow

Heaven never helps the man who will not act.

-Sophocles

There is no duty we so much underrate as the duty of being happy. By being happy, we sow anonymous benefits upon the world which remain unknown even to ourselves or, when they are disclosed, surprise nobody so much as the benefactor.

-Robert Louis Stevenson

Be kind. Every man you meet is fighting a hard battle.

-Ian MacLaren

Study the unusually successful people you know and you will find them imbued with enthusiasm for their work, which is contagious. Not only are they themselves excited about what they are doing, but they also get you excited.

-Paul W. Ivey

Always dream and shoot higher than you know you can do. Don't bother just to be better than your contemporaries or predecessors. Try to be better than yourself.

-William Faulkner

Some people dream of worthy accomplishments while others stay awake and do them.

-Anonymous

Calmness of mind is one of the beautiful jewels of wisdom. It is the result of long and patient effort in self-control. Its presence is an indication of ripened experience and of a more than ordinary knowledge of the laws and operations of thought.

-James L. Allen

All human power is a compound of time and patience.

-Honore de Balzac

A word too much always defeats its purpose.

-Arthur Schopenhauer

It is expedient to have acquaintance with those who have looked into the world, who know men, understand business and can give you good intelligence and good advice when they are wanted.

-George Horne

The habit of being uniformly considerate toward others will bring increased happiness to you. As you put into practice the qualities of patience, punctuality, sincerity and solicitude, you will have a better opinion of the world about you.

-Grenville Kleiser

One of the greatest victories you can gain over a man is to beat him at politeness.

-Josh Billings

I have a room all to myself. It is nature. It is a place beyond the jurisdiction of human government.

-Anonymous

Happiness is not in our circumstances, but in ourselves. It is not something we see, like a rainbow, or feel, like the heat of a fire. Happiness is something we are.

-John B. Sheerin

Big shots are little shots who kept shooting.

-Christopher Morley

One should seek virtue for its own sake and not from hope or fear or any external motive. It is in virtue that happiness consists, for virtue is the state of mind which tends to make the whole of life harmonious.

-Zeno

The difference between a successful person and others is not a lack of strength, not a lack of knowledge, but rather in a lack of will.

-Anonymous

Wear your learning, like your watch, in a private pocket. Do not pull it out merely to show that you have one. If asked what o'clock it is, tell it; but do not proclaim it hourly and unasked, like the watchman.

-Lord Chesterfield

The best portion of a good man's life is his little, nameless, unremembered acts of kindness and of love.

-William Wordsworth

Real leaders are ordinary people with extraordinary determination.

-Anonymous

We can accomplish almost anything within our ability if we but think that we can! Every great achievement in this world was first carefully thought out. Think, but to a purpose. Think constructively. Think as you read. Think as you listen. Think as you travel and your eyes reveal new situations. Think as you work daily at your desk or in the field or while strolling. Think to rise and improve your place in life. There can be no advancement or success without serious thought.

-George Matthew Adams

Everything you say and do is a reflection of the inner you.

-Anonymous

It takes a lot of time to get experience, and once you have it you ought to go on using it.

-Benjamin M. Duggar

Never mind what others do. Do better than yourself. Beat your own record from day to day and you are a success.
-William J.H. Boetcker

In all human activities, particularly in all matters of business, times of stress and difficulty are seasons of opportunity when the seeds of progress are sown.
-Thomas F. Woodlock

By words we learn thoughts and by thoughts we learn life.
-Jean Baptiste Girard

Never shrink from doing anything which your business calls you to do. The man who is above his business may one day find his business above him.
-Samuel Drew

One of the most valuable things any man can learn is the art of using the knowledge and experience of others.
-Anonymous

Friendship is the only cement that will ever hold the world together.

-Woodrow Wilson

Sincerity and truth are the basis of every virtue.

-Confucius

Live and let live is not enough; live and help live is not too much.

-Orison Swett Marden

Most true happiness comes from one's inner life, from the disposition of the mind and soul. Admittedly, a good inner life is difficult to achieve, especially in these trying times. It takes reflection and contemplation and self-discipline.

-William L. Shirer

Unless we give part of ourselves away, unless we can live with other people and understand them and help them, we are missing the most essential part of our own human lives.

-Harold Taylor

Until you have learned to be tolerant with those who do not always agree with you; until you have cultivated the habit of saying some kind word of those whom you do not admire; until you have formed the habit of looking for the good instead of the bad there is in others; you will be neither successful nor happy.

-Anonymous

Your imagination has much to do with your life. It pictures beauty, success, desired results. On the other hand, it brings into focus ugliness, distress, and failure. It is for you to decide how you want your imagination to serve you.

-Philip Conley

It is difficult to live in the present, ridiculous to live in the future, and impossible to live in the past.

-Jim Bishop

Wisdom, itself, is often an abstraction associated not with fact or reality, but with the man who asserts it and the manner of its assertion.

-John Kenneth Galbraith

The way to be nothing is to do nothing.
-Edgar Watson Howe

There's no music in *rest,* but there's the making of music in it. And people are always missing that part of the life melody, always talking of perseverance and courage and fortitude, but patience is the finest and worthiest part of fortitude and the rarest, too.
-John Ruskin

The men who build the future are those who know that greater things are yet to come and that they themselves will help bring them about. Their minds are illumined by the blazing sun of hope. They never stop to doubt. They haven't time.
-Melvin J. Evans

There is nothing wrong with having nothing to say unless you insist on saying it.
-Anonymous

No duty is more urgent than that of returning thanks.
-St. Ambrose

The more one tries to teach a subject, the more he learns about that subject.

-Anonymous

Courage is the first of human qualities because it is the quality which guarantees all the others.

-Winston S. Churchill

No virtue is more universally accepted as a test of good character than trustworthiness.

-Harry Emerson Fosdick

If the world is cold, make it your business to build fires.

-Horace Traubel

How poor are they who have not patience! What wound did ever heal but by degrees.

-William Shakespeare

It's faith in something and enthusiasm for something that makes life worth looking at.

-Oliver Wendell Holmes

Man cannot be satisfied with mere success. He is concerned with the terms upon which success comes to him. And very often the terms seem more important than the success.

-Charles A. Bennett

What helps luck is a habit of watching for opportunities, of having a patient but restless mind, of sacrificing one's ease or vanity, of uniting a love of detail to foresight and of passing through hard times bravely and cheerfully.

-Charles Victor Cherbuliez

Do not anticipate trouble or worry about what may never happen. Keep in the sunlight.

-Benjamin Franklin

People are always blaming their circumstances for what they are. I don't believe in circumstances. People who get on in this world are the people who get up and look for the circumstances they want and, if they can't find them, they make them.

-Anonymous

It's good to have money and the things that money can buy, but it's good too, to check up once in a while and make sure that you haven't lost the things that money can't buy.

-George Horace Lorimer

The love of study, a passion which derives fresh vigor from enjoyment, supplies each day and hour with a perpetual source of independent and rational pleasure.

-Edward Gibbon

In the end, the only people who fail are those who do not try.

-Anonymous

Don't waste good thoughts on yesterday nor on days yet to come, but think good thoughts on things at hand and strive to make things hum. For now, today, is full of hope and pleasures we'll soon taste. If we will concentrate on now and precious time not waste.

-Alonzo Newton Benn

The sages do not consider that making no mistakes is a blessing. They believe, rather, that the great virtue of man lies in his ability to correct his mistakes and continually make a new man of himself.

-Wang Yang-Ming

Indecision is debilitating. It feeds upon itself. It is, one might almost say, habit-forming. Not only that, but it is contagious; it transmits itself to others. Business is dependent upon action. It cannot go forward by hesitation. Those in executive positions must fortify themselves with facts and accept responsibility for decisions based upon them. Often, greater risk is involved in postponement than in making a wrong decision.

-Harry A. Hopf

The race for quality has no finish line.

-Anonymous

Mistakes occur when a man is overworked or overconfident.

-William Feather

Apathy can only be overcome by enthusiasm and enthusiasm can only be aroused by two things: first, an ideal which takes the imagination by storm; and second, a definite intelligible plan for carrying that ideal into practice.

-Arnold Toynbee

It is our relation to circumstances that determines their influence over us. The same wind that carries one vessel into port may blow another off shore.

-Christian Bovee

Let us be thankful for the fools. But for them, the rest of us could not succeed.

-Anonymous

Anxiety is the poison of human life, the parent of many sins and of more miseries. In a world where everything is doubtful and where we may be disappointed and be blessed in disappointment, why this restless stir and commotion of mind? Can it alter the cause or unravel the mystery of human events?

-Paxton Blair

Excellence is an art won by training and habituation. We do not act rightly because we have virtue or excellence, but we rather have those because we have acted rightly. We are what we repeatedly do. Excellence, then, is not an act but a habit.

-Aristotle

Try to forget yourself in the service of others. For when we think too much of ourselves and our own interests, we easily become despondent. But, when we work for others, our efforts return to bless us.

-Sidney Powell

The race is not always to the swift, but to those who keep on running.

-Anonymous

The successful person is one who is able to take his talents and invest them in the business of living in a manner that leads to the accomplishment of a full life of service. The medium of exchange is not the dollar, but services rendered.

-Sol Roth

That you may retain your self-respect, it is better to displease the people by doing what you know is right than to temporarily please them by doing what you know is wrong.

-William J.H. Boetcker

Whether you be man or woman, you will never do anything in this world without courage. It is the greater quality of the mind next to honor.

-James L. Allen

The wisdom of the wise and the experience of ages may be preserved by quotation.

-Benjamin Disraeli

You'll always miss 100% of the shots you don't make.

-Anonymous

Confidence is that feeling by which the mind embarks in great and honorable courses with a sure hope and trust in itself.

-Cicero

Research is nothing but a state of mind, a friendly, welcoming attitude toward change; going out to look for a change instead of waiting for it to come. Research, for practical men, is an effort to do things better. The research state of mind can apply to anything, personal affairs of any kind of business, big or little.

-Charles F. Kettering

You will never *find* time for anything. If you want time you must *make it.*

-Charles Buxton

Accustom yourself to master and overcome things of difficulty; for if you observe, the left hand for want of practice is insignificant and not adapted to general business, yet it holds the bridle better that the right, from constant use.

-Pliny

We cannot direct the wind, but we can adjust the sails.

-Anonymous

Be not too presumptuously sure in any business; for things of this world depend on such a train of unseen chances that if it were in man's hands to set the tables, still he would not be certain to win the game.

-Lord Herbert

Some relaxation is necessary to people of every degree; the head that thinks and the hand that labors must have some little time to recruit their diminished powers.

-Bernard Gilpin

A positive attitude overcomes even the biggest obstacles.

-Anonymous

Real intelligence is a creative use of knowledge, not merely an accumulation of facts. The slow thinker who can finally come up with an idea of his own is more important to the world than a walking encyclopedia who hasn't learned how to use information productively.

-D. Kenneth Winebrenner

Happiness consists more in small conveniences or pleasures that occur every day than in great pieces of good fortune that happen but seldom to a man in the course of his life.

-Benjamin Franklin

The difference between intelligence and an education is this: that intelligence will make you a good living.

-Charles F. Kettering

Property may be destroyed and money may lose its purchasing power; but character, health, knowledge and good judgment will always be in demand under all conditions.

-Roger Babson

If we don't take care of the customer, somebody else will.

-Anonymous

A superior man is the one who is free from fear and anxieties.

-Confucius

Our success or our failure is the result of our mental condition; our thoughts about people and about ourselves; our attitudes toward people and toward ourselves.

-Dan Custer

We can't always control what happens to us. But we can control what we think about what happens. And what we are thinking is our *life* at any particular moment.

-Norman G. Shidle

Man is not the creature of circumstances, circumstances are the creatures of men.

-Anonymous

The best education in the world is that got by struggling to get a living.

-Wendell Phillips

Wisdom comes not from experience, but from meditating on experience and assimilating it.

-Joy Elmer Morgan

It takes wit and interest and energy to be happy. The pursuit of happiness is a great activity. One must be open and alive. It is the greatest feat man has to accomplish, and spirits must flow. There must be courage. There are no easy ruts to get into which lead to happiness. A man must become interesting to himself and must become actually expressive before he can be happy.

-Robert Henri

Each new development starts from something else. It does not come out of a blue sky. You make use of that which has already entered the mind. That is the real reason for accumulating knowledge.

-Robert P. Crawford

True success is the only thing that you cannot have unless and until you have offered it to others.

-Sri Chinmoy

Keep your face to the sunshine and you cannot see the shadows.

-Anonymous

Follow your own path no matter what people say.
-Karl Marx

I often wonder why people do not make more of the marvelous power there is in kindness. It is the greatest lever to move the hearts of men that the world has ever known, greater by far than anything that mere ingenuity can devise or subtlety suggest. Kindness is the kingpin of success in life; it is the prime factor in overcoming friction and making the human machinery run smoothly.
-Andrew Chapman

If you want to succeed in the world, you must make your own opportunities as you go on. The man who waits for some seventh wave to toss him onto dry land will find that the seventh wave is a long time coming.
-John B. Gough

Don't let life discourage you; everyone who got where he is had to begin where he was.
-Richard L. Evans

Never mind what the people think of you! They may overestimate or underestimate you! Until they discover your real worth, your success depends mainly upon what you think of yourself and whether you believe in yourself. You can succeed if nobody else believes it; but you will never succeed if you don't believe in yourself.

-William J.H. Boetcker

Sooner or later, a man, if he is wise, discovers that life is a mixture of good days and bad, victory and defeat, give and take.

-Wilfred A. Peterson

You have not lived a perfect day, even though you have earned your money, unless you have done something for someone who will never be able to repay you.

-Ruth Smeltzer

The mind that is anxious about the future is miserable.

-Seneca

Twenty years from now you will be more disappointed by the things you didn't do than by the ones you did. So, throw off the bowlines. Sail away from the safe harbor. Catch the trade winds in your sails. *Explore. Dream. Discover.*

-Anonymous

The art of dealing with people is the foremost secret of successful men. A man's success in handling people is the very yardstick by which the outcome of his whole life's work is measured.

-Paul C. Packer

There are people who are always anticipating trouble and, in this way, they manage to enjoy many sorrows that never really happen to them.

-Josh Billings

Far away there in the sunshine are my highest aspirations. I may not reach them, but I can look up and see their beauty, believe in them and try to follow where they lead.

-Louisa May Alcott

Man is not the creature of circumstances, circumstances are the creatures of man. We are free agents and man is more powerful than matter.

-Benjamin Disraeli

It is not love of self but hatred of self which is at the root of the troubles that afflict our world.

-Eric Hoffer

Consider how hard it is to change yourself and you'll understand what little chance you have trying to change others.

-Arnold Glasow

A consistent man believes in destiny, a capricious man in chance.

-Anonymous

One is wasting life force every time he talks of failure, of hard luck, of troubles and trials, of past errors and mistakes. Let him turn his back on the past and face the light.

-Orison Swett Marden

By struggling with misfortunes, we are sure to receive some wounds in the conflict; but a sure method to come off victorious is by running away.

-Oliver Goldsmith

Regardless of circumstances, each man lives in a world of his own making.

-Joseph Murray Emms

Life is growth, a challenge of environment. If we cannot meet our everyday surroundings with equanimity and pleasure and grow each day in some useful direction, then this splendid balance of cosmic forces which we call life is on the road toward misfortune, misery and destruction. Therefore, health is the most precious of all things.

-Luther Burbank

High, but not the highest intelligence, combined with the greatest degree of persistence, will achieve greater eminence than the highest degree of intelligence without somewhat less persistence.

-Catherine M. Cox

To be successful, you've got to be willing to fail.
-Frank Tyger

No one rises so high as he who knows not whither he is going.
-Oliver Cromwell

Teach the young people how to think, not what to think.
-Sidney Sugarman

Behavior is a mirror in which everyone shows his image.
-Goethe

Have no fear of change as such and, on the other hand, no liking for it merely for its own sake.
-Robert Moses

Every human mind is a great slumbering power until awakened by keen desire and by definite resolution to do.
-Edgar R. Roberts

It is where a man spends his money that shows where his heart lies.

-A. Edwin Keigwin

No man can rise to fame or fortune without carrying others along with him.

-Anonymous

To be ambitious for wealth and yet always expecting to be poor; to be always doubting your ability to get what you long for is like trying to reach east by traveling west. There is no philosophy which will help man to succeed when he is always doubting his ability to do so and thus attracting failure. No matter how hard you work for success, if your thought is saturated with the fear of failure, it will kill your efforts, neutralize your endeavors and make success impossible.

-Charles Baudouin

Fear not that thy life shall come to an end, but rather fear that it shall never have a beginning.

-John Henry Newman

Wisdom, compassion and courage; these are three universally recognized moral qualities of man. It matters not in what way men come to the exercise of these moral qualities, the result is one and the same. When a man understands the nature and use of these three moral qualities, he will then understand how to put in order his personal conduct and character, he will understand how to govern men. When a man understands how to govern men, he will then understand how to govern nations and empires.

-Confucius

We are rich only through what we give; and poor only through what we refuse and keep.

-Anne Swetchine

Take spring when it comes and rejoice. Take happiness when it comes and rejoice. Take love when it comes and rejoice.

-Carl Ewald

To suffer and to endure is the lot of humanity.

-Pope Leo XIII

If you love knowledge, you will be a master of knowledge. What you have come to know, pursue by exercise; what you have not learned, seek to add to your knowledge, for it is as reprehensible to hear a profitable saying and not grasp it, as to be offered a good gift by one's friends and not accept it. Believe that many precepts are better than much wealth, for wealth quickly fails us, but precepts abide through all time.

-Socrates

Ninety percent of the art of living consists of getting on with people one cannot stand.

-Samuel Goldwyn

This is a world of action and not for moping and droning in.

-Charles Dickens

There are two things needed in these days; first, for rich men to find out how poor men live; and second, for poor men to know how rich men work.

-John Foster

If we would keep filling our minds with the picture of happy things ahead, many of the worries and anxieties and perhaps ill health would naturally melt away. If we lived in the atmosphere of expectancy, so many of our petty problems would be no problems at all. Always expect the best. Then if you have to hurdle a few tough problems, you will have generated the strength and courage to do so. Successful businesses are forever planning and dreaming ahead, and so should we, as individuals. Expect to discover the best in people and they will do the same for you. We must be constructive in our thoughts and our attitude toward life.

-George Matthew Adams

Every individual should have a purpose in life which is worthy of intense effort and constantly work toward the definite goal ahead.

-Roderick Stevens

It isn't the size of the dog in the fight, but the size of the fight in the dog that counts.

-Woody Hayes

Grant me the serenity to accept the things I cannot change, the courage to change the things I can and the wisdom to know the difference.

-Reinhold Niebuhr

Nothing gives one person so much advantage over another as to remain cool and unruffled under all circumstances.

-Thomas Jefferson

I've never known a man worth his salt who in the long run, deep down in his heart, didn't appreciate the grind, the discipline. I firmly believe that any man's finest hour, this greatest fulfillment to all he holds dear, is that moment when he has worked his heart out in a good cause and lies exhausted on the field of battle victorious.

-Vincent T. Lombardi

The men who try to do something and fail are infinitely better than those who try nothing and succeed.

-Lloyd Jones

Victories that are easy are cheap. Those only are worth having which come as the result of hard work.

-Henry Ward Beecher

True wisdom comes from the overcoming of suffering and sin. All true wisdom is therefore touched with sadness.

-Whittaker Chambers

Timing is everything. It is important to know when, as to know how.

-Arnold Glasow

You can't build a reputation on what you are going to do.

-Henry Ford

To avoid criticism do nothing, say nothing, be nothing.

-Elbert Hubbard

Whether you think you can or you can't, you're right.

-Anonymous

It is not for man to rest in absolute contentment. He is born to hopes and aspirations.

-Robert Southey

We first make our habits and then our habits make us.

-Anonymous

The very substance of the ambitious is merely the shadow of a dream.

-William Shakespeare

Blessed is the man that has found his work. One monster there is in the world, the idle man.

-Thomas Carlyle

Successful salesmen, authors, executives and workmen of every sort need patience. The great liability of youth is not inexperience, but impatience.

-William Feather

A strong imagination beggeth opportunity.

-Michel Eyquem De Montaigne

The deed is everything, the glory naught.
-Johann Wolfgang Von Goethe

Make your plans as fantastic as you like, because 25 years from now they will seem mediocre. Make your plans ten times as great as you first planned and 25 years from now you will wonder why you did not make them 50 times as great.
-Henry Curtis

Faith in your own powers and confidence in your individual methods are essential to success.
-Roderick Stevens

Most barriers to your success are man made. And most often, you're the man who made them.
-Frank Tyger

It is better to do the wrong thing than to do nothing.
-Winston S. Churchill

Wealth is the result of effective evaluations.
-Anonymous

There is an island of opportunity in the middle of every difficulty.

-Anonymous

Beware what you set your heart upon. For it surely shall be yours.

-Ralph Waldo Emerson

One good head is better than a hundred strong hands.

-Thomas Fuller

A purpose is the eternal condition of success.

-Theodore T. Munger

Money is like love; it kills slowly and painfully the one who withholds it and it enlivens the other who turns it upon his fellow man.

-Kahlil Gibran

High station in life is earned by the gallantry with which appalling experiences are survived with grace.

-Tennessee Williams

The happiness of your life depends upon the quality of your thoughts.

-Marcus Aurelius Antoninus

A successful life is not an easy life. It is built upon strong qualities, sacrifice, endeavor, loyalty, integrity.

-Grant D. Brandon

The first great gift we can bestow on others is a good example.

-Thomas Morell

He who knows no guilt knows no fear.

-Philip Massinger

The only conquests which are permanent and leave no regrets are our conquests over ourselves.

-Napoleon Bonaparte

Most people say that as you get old, you have to give up things. I think you get old because you give up things.

-Theodore Francis Green

Speak not but what may benefit others or yourself; avoid trifling conversation.

-Benjamin Franklin

Conversation means being able to disagree and still continue the conversation.

-Dwight MacDonald

Hearing is one of the body's five senses. But listening is an art.

-Frank Tyger

The earnestness of your desire will indicate the distance you are likely to travel.

-Clark C. Stockford

If you would only recognize that life is hard, things would be so much easier for you.

-Louis D. Brandeis

Do today what should be done. Your tomorrow may never come.

-Harry F. Banks

Contentment is not happiness. An oyster may be contented.

-Christian Bovee

Satisfaction of one's curiosity is one of the greatest sources of happiness in life.

-Linus Pauling

In the race to be better or best, do not miss the joy of being.

-Anonymous

Even in social life, it is persistency which attracts confidence more than talents and accomplishments.

-Edwin P. Whipple

The price of greatness is responsibility.

-Winston S. Churchill

The line between failure and success is so fine that we scarcely know when we pass it; so fine that we often are on the line and do not know it.

-Ralph Waldo Emerson

Success is often just an idea away.

-Frank Tyger

Knowledge is the antidote to fear.

-Ralph Waldo Emerson

God gave us our memories so that we might have roses in December.

-James M. Barrie

Conceit is the quicksand of success.

-Arnold Glasow

If you mean to profit, learn to please.

-Winston S. Churchill

What comes with ease, goes with ease.

-Arabian Proverb

Enthusiasm is the mainspring of the soul. Keep it wound up and you will never be without power to get what you actually need.

-Anonymous

In life, as in football, you won't go far unless you know where the goal posts are.

-Arnold Glasow

When in doubt, tell the truth.

-Mark Twain

We lift ourselves by our thought; we climb upon our vision of ourselves.

-Anonymous

The shell must break before the bird can fly.

-Alfred Lord Tennyson

There is no shame in having fallen, nor any shame in being born into a lowly estate. There is only shame in not struggling to rise and, also, shame for not wishing to attain the better or not dreaming about and praying for it.

-Samuel Amalu

Happiness is more a state of health than of wealth.

-Frank Tyger

Those who know, do not tell; those who tell, do not know.
-Lao-Tse

Success won't just come to you. It has to be met at least halfway.
-Frank Tyger

Most men talk too much. Much of my success has been due to keeping my mouth shut.
-J. Ogden Armour

A true friend never gets in your way unless you happen to be going down.
-Arnold Glasow

Attitude is a little thing that makes a big difference.
-Anonymous

Enthusiasm is at the bottom of all progress. With it, there is accomplishment. Without it, there are only alibis.
-Henry Ford

Press on. Nothing in the world can take the place of persistence.

-Ray A. Kroc

Tact is the great ability to see other people as they think you see them.

-Carl Zuckmayer

What is happiness? The feeling that power increases; that resistance is overcome.

-Friedrich W. Nietzsche

One never finds life worth living. One always has to *make* life worth living.

-Harry Emerson Fosdick

The gent who wakes up and finds himself a success hasn't been asleep.

-Wilson Mizner

I will study and get ready and someday my chance will come.

-Abraham Lincoln

There is the true joy of life: to be used by a purpose recognized by yourself as a mighty one; to be thoroughly worn out before being thrown on the scrap heap; to be a force of nature instead of a feverish, selfish little clod of ailments and grievances complaining that life will not devote itself to making you happy.

-George Bernard Shaw

Your only limits are the size of your ideas and the degree of your dedication.

-Anonymous

There is no remedy for love but to love more.

-Henry David Thoreau

Why is one man richer than another? Because he is more industrious, more persevering and more sagacious.

-John Ruskin

A jack-of-all-trades is king of none.

-P.K. Thomajan

There is no force so democratic as the force of an ideal.
-Calvin Coolidge

We work to become, not to acquire.
-Elbert Hubbard

Doubts and jealousies often beget the facts they fear.
-Thomas Jefferson

There is always hope for an individual who stops to do some serious thinking about life.
-Katherine Logan

It takes both rain and sunshine to make a rainbow.
-Anonymous

To get your ideas across, use small words, big ideas and short sentences.
-John Henry Patterson

Only a life lived for others is a life worthwhile.
-Albert Einstein

Hide not your talents, they for use were made. What's a sundial in the shade?

-Benjamin Franklin

Even as we speak, jealous time flees; seize this day and put little faith in tomorrow.

-Horace

The most destructive criticism is indifference.

-Edgar Watson Howe

The path of least resistance is what makes rivers run crooked.

-Elbert Hubbard

Ability is useless unless it's used.

-Robert Half

There is more self-love than love in jealousy.

-Francois La Rochefoucauld

Keep your mouth shut and your eyes open.

-Samuel Palmer

I like the dreams of the future better than the history of the past.

-Thomas Jefferson

Whatever is worth doing at all is worth doing well.

-Philip Dormer Stanhope &
-Lord Chesterfield

To think of learning as a preparation for something beyond learning is a defeat of the process. The most important attitude that can be formed is that of desire to go on learning.

-Daniel Bell

The heights by great men reached and kept were not attained by sudden flight, but they, while their companions slept, were toiling upward in the night.

-Henry Wadsworth Longfellow

It is well worth remembering that the customer is the most important factor in any business. If you don't think so, try getting along without him for awhile.

-Anonymous

*Self-love* is the instrument of our preservation. It resembles the provision for the reproduction of mankind. It is necessary. It gives us pleasure and we must conceal it

-Francois Marie Arouet Voltaire

Ninety-eight out of 100 of the rich men in America are honest. That is why they are rich.

-Russell Herman Conwell

It is not death that a man should fear, but he should fear never beginning to live.

-Marcus Aurelius Antoninus

Happiness is a by-product of an effort to make someone else happy.

-Gretta Palmer

As long as the day lasts, let's give it all we got.

-David O. McKay

The world belongs to the energetic.

-Ralph Waldo Emerson

No one can make you feel inferior without your consent.
-Eleanor Roosevelt

Slow and steady wins the race.
-Anonymous

The greatest service we can perform for others is to help them to help themselves.
-Horace Mann

The strength of a man's virtue must not be measured by his occasional efforts, but by his ordinary life.
-Blaise Pascal

We must not sit down and wait for miracles. Up and be going!
-John Elliot

I've never been poor, only broke. Being poor is a frame of mind. Being broke is only a temporary situation.
-Mike Todd

Don't be afraid to take a big step if one is indicated. You can't cross a chasm in two small jumps.

-David Lloyd George

Seize this very minute! What you can do, or think you can do, begin it!

-Johann Wolfgang von Goethe

Nothing will ever be attempted if all possible objections must be first overcome.

-Samuel Johnson

The making of money, the accumulation of material power, is not all there is to living. Life is something more than these and the man who misses this truth misses the greatest joy and satisfaction that can come into his life service for others.

-Edward W. Bok

As soon as a preoccupation with security begins to dominate human life, the scope of human life itself tends to be diminished.

-Gabriel Marcel

There is no fear without some hope, and no hope without some fear.

-Baruch Spinoza

The time to relax is when you don't have time for it.

-Sydney J. Harris

It is a beautiful and blessed world we live in, and while life lasts, to lose the enjoyment of it is a sin.

-A.W. Chambers

A man doesn't need brilliance or genius. All he needs is energy.

-Albert M. Greenfield

Patience and time do more than strength or passion.

-Jean De La Fontaine

He that has no patience has nothing at all.

-Italian Proverb

Manners make often fortunes.

-John Ray

Along with success comes a reputation for wisdom.
-Euripides

A wise man will make tools of what comes to hand.
-Thomas Fuller

Self-respect: that cornerstone of all virtue.
-John Herschel

By failing to prepare, you are preparing to fail.
-Benjamin Franklin

Giving up is the ultimate tragedy.
-Robert J. Donovan

Nobody succeeds in a big way except by risking failure.
-William Feather

Regret for the things we did can be tempered by time; it is regret for the things we did not do that is inconsolable.
-Sydney J. Harris

Lack of will power and drive cause more failures than lack of intelligence and ability.

-Harry F. Banks

No mistake or failure is as bad as to stop and not try again.

-John Wanamaker

I cannot change yesterday. I can only make the most of today, and look with hope toward tomorrow.

-Anonymous

Courage is grace under pressure.

-Ernest Hemingway

Philosophy is the art of living.

-Plutarch

You have to leave the city of your comfort and go into the wilderness of your intuition. What you will discover will be wonderful. What you will discover will be yourself.

-Alan Alda

The great aim of education is not knowledge, but action.
-Herbert Spencer

The right man is the one who seizes the moment.
-Johann Wolfgang Von Goethe

Pleasure and pain are the only springs of action in man and always will be.
-Claude Helvetius

Enthusiasm is the greatest asset in the world. It beats money and power and influence.
-Henry Chester

Winning isn't everything, but wanting to win is.
-Vincent T. Lombardi

Impatience never commanded success.
-Edwin H. Chapin

Patience is the companion of wisdom.
-St. Augustine

Our greatest glory is not in never falling, but in rising every time we fall.

-Confucius

What you can Conceive and Believe you can *Achieve* with *Positive Mental Attitude.*

-Anonymous

A person who is not disturbed by the incessant flow of desires that enter like rivers into the ocean, which is ever being filled but is always still, can alone achieve peace, and not the man who strives to satisfy such desires.

-Bhagavad Gita

Perhaps wisdom is to be found in people who have suffered greatly, but have surmounted it.

-Louis Jolyon West

We act as though comfort and luxury were the chief requirements of life when all that we need to make us happy is something to be enthusiastic about.

-Charles Kingsley

Whether it's marriage or business, patience is the first rule of success.

-William Feather

He conquers who conquers himself.

-Latin Proverb

We need not seek opportunity in the distance. We may find it right where we stand.

-Anonymous

Believe that life is worth living and your belief will help create the fact.

-William James

They can conquer who believe they can.

-William Dryden

There is a master key to success with which no man can fail. Its name is simplicity. Whenever I have met a business proposition which, after taking thought, I could not reduce to simplicity, I have left it alone.

-Henry Detering

To be without some of the things you want is an indispensable part of happiness.

-Bertrand Russell

Happiness is a dividend on a well-invested life.

-Duncan Stuart

The only way to get happiness is by giving it away to others.

-Anonymous

Nothing is impossible to the man who can will.

-Honore De Mirabeau

Life unexamined is not worth living.

-Democritus

The most exquisite paradox is that as soon as you give it all up, you can have it all. As long as you want power, you can't have it. The minute you don't want power, you'll have more than you ever dreamed possible.

-Ram Dass

There is no misfortune, but to bear it nobly is good fortune.

-Marcus Aurelius Antoninus

The purpose of life is to believe, to hope and to strive.

-Indira Gandhi

If at first you don't succeed, try hard work.

-William Feather

Hold fast to dreams, for if dreams die, life is a broken-winged bird that cannot fly.

-Langston Hughes

The growth of wisdom may be gauged accurately by the decline of ill temper.

-Friedrich W. Nietzsche

Our greatest pretenses are built up not to hide the evil and the ugly in us, but our emptiness. The hardest thing to hide is something that is not there.

-Eric Hoffer

He that is master of himself will soon be master of others.
-H.G. Bohn

Life is what happens to you while you are making other plans.
-Anonymous

Life's more than a magazine in which we flip the pages and enjoy the pictures.
-Ralph Boyer

Protect your health. Without it you face a serious handicap for success and happiness.
-Harry F. Banks

Courage conquers all things.
-Ovid

The world is moving so fast these days that the man who says it can't be done is generally interrupted by someone doing it.
-Harry Emerson Fosdick

People don't like to hear stories about your troubles. They have a whole flock of their own.

-Anonymous

Men are born to succeed, not to fail.

-David Henry Thoreau

Keep on going and the chances are you will stumble on something, perhaps when you are least expecting it. I have never heard of anyone stumbling on something sitting down.

-Charles F. Kettering

I once complained to my father that I didn't seem to be able to do things the same way other people did. Dad's advice? "Margo, don't be a sheep. People hate sheep. They eat sheep."

-Margo Kaufman

Fortunate is the person who has learned that the most certain way to *get* is to first *give* through some sort of useful service

-Napoleon Hill

The thing I fear most is fear.

-Michel Eyquem De Montaigne

Fear is that little darkroom where negatives are developed.

-Michael Pritchard

Do not fear death so much, but rather the inadequate life.

-Bertolt Brecht

Fear fades when facts are faced.

-Frank Tyger

It's all right to have butterflies in your stomach. Just get them to fly in formation.

-Dr. Rob Gilbert

Pleasure is a shadow, wealth is a vanity and power is a pageant; but knowledge is ecstatic in enjoyment, perennial in frame, unlimited in space and infinite in duration.

-DeWitt Clinton

One doesn't discover new lands without consenting to lose sight of the shore for a very long time.
-Andre Gide

Defeat, like a headache, warns us that something has gone wrong. If we are intelligent we look for the cause and profit by the experience.
-Napoleon Hill

Courage is doing what you're afraid to do. There can be no courage unless you're scared.
-Eddie Rickenbacker

The ancestor of every action is a thought.
-Ralph Waldo Emerson

It will make a real difference to you if you are a person with a message or a person with a grievance.
-Anonymous

Our doubts are traitors and make us lose the good we oft might win by fearing to attempt.
-William Shakespeare

He not busy being born is busy dying.
-Bob Dylan

When love and skill work together, expect a masterpiece.
-John Ruskin

The way you activate the seeds of your creation is by making choices about the results you want to create. When you make a choice, you mobilize vast human energies and resources which otherwise go untapped. All too often people fail to focus their choices upon results and therefore their choices are ineffective. If you limit your choices only to what seems possible or reasonable, you disconnect yourself from what you truly want and all that is left is a compromise.
-Robert Fritz

You've got to create a dream. You've got to uphold the dream. If you can't, go back to the factory or go back to the desk.
-Eric Burdon

If a man does his best, what else is there?
-Anonymous

The truth is that all of us attain the greatest success and happiness possible in this life whenever we use our native capacities to their greatest extent.
-Dr. Smiley Blanton

Advice is what we ask for when we already know the answer, but wish we didn't.
-Erica Jong

Here is the test to find whether your mission on earth is finished. If you're alive, it isn't.
-Richard Back

Losers visualize the penalties of failure. Winners visualize the rewards of success.
-Dr. Rob Gilbert

If you cannot save money, the seed of success is not in you.
-Anonymous

Ours is a world where people don't know what they want and are willing to go through hell to get it.
-Don Marquis

Passion is in all great searches and is necessary to all creative endeavors.
-W. Eugene Smith

The method of the enterprising is to plan with audacity and execute with vigor; to sketch out a map of possibilities; and then to treat them as probabilities.
-Christian Bovee

When you cease to make a contribution, you begin to die.
-Eleanor Roosevelt

You can have anything you want if you want it desperately enough. You must want it with an inner exuberance that erupts through the skin and joins the energy that created the world.
-Sheila Graham

There is no defeat except from within.
-Anonymous

Guilt is never a rational thing; it distorts all the faculties of the human mind, it perverts them, it leaves a man no longer in the free use of his reason, it puts him into confusion.
-Edmund Burke

Be bold and mighty forces will come to your aid.
-Basil King

Experience is not what happens to a man; it is what a man does with what happens to him.
-Anonymous

It's surprising how many persons go through life without ever recognizing that their feelings toward other people are largely determined by their feelings toward themselves and, if you're not comfortable within yourself, you can't be comfortable with others.
-Sydney J. Harris

To be nobody but yourself in a world which is doing its best day and night to make you like everybody else means to fight the hardest battle which any human being can fight and never stop fighting.

-e.e. cummings

I bargained with life for a penny and life would pay no more. However, I begged at evening when I counted my scanty store. For life is a just employer, it gives you what you ask. But once you have set the wages, why, you must bear the task. I worked for a menial's hire, only to learn, dismayed, that any wage I had asked of life, life would have willingly paid.

-Napoleon Hill

We should be taught not to wait for inspiration to start a thing. Action always generates inspiration. Inspiration seldom generates action.

-Frank Tibolt

The essential conditions of everything you do must be choice, love, passion.

-Nadia Boulanger

I saw that all things I feared, and which feared me, had nothing good or bad in them save insofar as the mind was affected by them.

-Baruch Spinoza

The trouble with people who talk too fast is that they often say something they haven't thought of yet.

-Anonymous

The person who sows a single beautiful thought in the mind of another, renders the world a greater service than that rendered by all the faultfinders combined.

-Napoleon Hill

'Tis the good reader that makes the good book. In every book he finds passages which seem to be confidences or asides hidden from all else and unmistakably meant for his ear. The profit of books is according to the sensibility of the reader. The profoundest thought or passion sleeps as in a mine, until it is discovered by an equal mind and heart.

-Ralph Waldo Emerson

Live all you can; it's a mistake not to. It doesn't so much matter what you do in particular, so long as you have your life. If you haven't had that, what have you had? What one loses, one loses, make no mistake about that. The right time is any time that one is still so lucky as to have. Live!

-Henry James

Love is patient and kind. Love is not jealous or boastful. It is not arrogant or rude. Love does not insist on its own way. It is not irritable or resentful. It does not rejoice at wrong, but rejoices in the right. Love bears all things, believes all things, hopes all things, endures all things. Love never ends. As for prophecies, they will pass away. As for tongues, they will cease. As for knowledge, it will pass away. For our knowledge is imperfect and our prophecy is imperfect. But when the perfect comes, the imperfect will pass away.

-Corinthians 13: 1-9

Every adversity is usually a blessing in disguise.

-Anonymous

We become what we think about all day long.
-Ralph Waldo Emerson

Man's mind, stretched to a new idea, never goes back to its original dimension.
-Oliver Wendell Holmes

People and things do not upset us. Rather, we upset ourselves by believing that they can upset us.
-Albert Ellis

There is nothing either good or bad, but thinking makes it so.
-William Shakespeare

The quotations when engraved upon the memory give you good thoughts. They also make you anxious to read the authors and look for more.
-Winston S. Churchill

People are about as happy as they make up their mind to be.
-Abraham Lincoln

You have no problems, just challenges.
-Anonymous

Change your thoughts and you change your world.
-Norman Vincent Peale

Be not the slave of your own past. Plunge into the sublime seas, dive deep and swim far so you shall come back with self-respect, with new power, with an advanced experience that shall explain and overlook the old.
-Ralph Waldo Emerson

The test of first-rate intelligence is the ability to hold two opposed ideas in mind at the same time and still retain the ability to function. One should, for example, be able to see that things are hopeless and yet be determined to make them better.
-F. Scott Fitzgerald

The most important thing to do in solving a problem is to begin.
-Frank Tyger

Happiness is the supreme object of existence.

-J. Gilchrist Lawson

Great spirits have always encountered violent opposition from mediocre minds.

-Albert Einstein

It is hard to find an enemy who has outposts in your head.

-Sally Kempton

You catch more bees with honey than you do with vinegar.

-Anonymous

Forgiveness is the fragrance the violet sheds on the heel that has crushed it.

-Mark Twain

The way a book is read, which is to say, the qualities a reader brings to a book can have as much to do with its worth as anything the author puts into it.

-Norman Cousins

To love oneself is the beginning of a lifelong romance.
-Oscar Wilde

Strong lives are motivated by dynamic purposes.
-Kenneth Hildebrand

Determination today leads to success tomorrow.
-Anonymous

The man who tried his best and failed is superior to the man who never tried.
-Bud Wilkinson

The wise man sees in the misfortunes of others what he should avoid.
-Publilius Syrus

Knowledge doesn't pay; it is what you do with it.
-Arnold Glasow

Common sense is not so common.
-Francois Marie Arouet Voltaire

A human being is a part of the whole called by us *Universe,* a part limited in time and space. He experiences himself, his thoughts and feelings, as something separated from the rest, a kind of optical delusion of his consciousness. This delusion is a kind of prison for us, restricting us to our personal desires and to affection for a few persons nearest to us. Our task must be to free ourselves from this prison by widening our circle of compassion to embrace all living creatures and the whole nature in its beauty.

-Albert Einstein

I couldn't wait for success, so I went ahead without it.

-Anonymous

In spite of *illness,* in spite even of the archenemy *sorrow,* one can remain alive long past the usual date of disintegration if one is unafraid of change, insatiable in intellectual curiosity, interested in big things, and happy in small ways.

-Edith Wharton

Build your weaknesses until they become your strengths.
-Anonymous

We are perhaps, uniquely among the earth's creatures, the worrying animal. We worry away our lives, fearing the future, discontent with the present, unable to take in the idea of dying, unable to sit still.
-Lewis Thomas

Every good thought you think is contributing its share to the ultimate result of your life.
-Grenville Kleiser

The mind is its own place, and in itself can make heaven of Hell, a hell of Heaven.
-Milton

We are wide-eyed in contemplating the possibility that life may exist elsewhere in the universe, but we wear blinders when contemplating the possibilities of life on earth.
-Norman Cousins

Enlighten the people generally, and tyranny and oppressions of body and mind will vanish like evil spirits at the dawn of the day.

-Thomas Jefferson

Aspiration is greater than realization because it keeps us eternally climbing upward toward some unattained goal.

-Anonymous

Great men are they who see that spiritual is stronger than any material force, that thoughts rule the world.

-Ralph Waldo Emerson

It is common sense to take a method and try it. If it fails, admit it frankly and try another. But, above all, try something.

-Franklin D. Roosevelt

Who knows? Maybe my life belongs to God. Maybe it belongs to me. But I do know one thing, I'm damned if it belongs to the government.

-Arthur Hoppe

The strangest and most fantastic fact about negative emotions is that people actually worship them.

-P.D. Ouspensky

Remember that the *kite of success* generally rises against the *wind of adversity,* not with it.

-Anonymous

Attachment is the great fabricator of illusions; reality can be attained only by someone who is detached.

-Simone Weil

Perseverance and audacity generally win.

-Dorothee' Luzy

I believe that anyone can conquer fear by doing the things he fears to do provided he keeps doing them until he gets a record of successful experiences behind him.

-Eleanor Roosevelt

He who has a *why* to live can bear almost any *how.*

-Friedrich W. Nietzsche

The apprehension of the good gives but the greater feeling to the worse.

-William Shakespeare

I cannot give you the formula for success, but I can give you the formula for failure which is: *Try to please everybody.*

-Herbert Bayard Swope

One should sympathize with the joy, the beauty, the color of life. The less said about life's sores, the better.

-Oscar Wilde

Great achievement is usually born of great sacrifice and is never the result of selfishness.

-Anonymous

*Do all the good* you can, *by all the means* you can, *in all the ways* you can, *in all the places* you can, *at all the times* you can, *to all the people* you can, *as long as ever* you can.

-John Wesley

Accept the challenges so that you may feel the exhilaration of victory.

-Anonymous

Until one is committed, there is hesitancy, the chance to draw back, always ineffectiveness. Concerning all acts of initiative (and creation) there is one elementary truth, the ignorance of which kills countless ideas and splendid plans; that the moment one definitely commits oneself, then Providence moves too. All sorts of things occur to help one that would never otherwise have occurred. A whole stream of events issues from the decision, raising in one's favor all manner of unforeseen incidents and meetings and material assistance which no man could have dreamed would have come his way. I have learned a deep respect for one of Goethe's couplets: *Whatever you can do, or dream you can, begin it. Boldness has genius power and magic in it.*

-W.H. Murray

Love truth, but pardon error.

-Francois Marie Arouet Voltaire

Fear no man, hate no man, wish no one misfortune and more than likely you will have plenty of friends.

-Anonymous

An optimist may see a light where there is none, but why must the pessimist always run to blow it out?

-Michel De Saint-Pierre

Death is not the greatest loss in life. The greatest loss is what dies inside us while we live.

-Norman Cousins

We can change our whole life and the attitude of people around us simply by changing ourselves.

-Rudolf Driekurs

The spirit of self-help is the root of all genuine growth in the individual; and, exhibited in the lives of many, it constitutes the true source of national vigor and strength. Help from without is often enfeebling in its effects, but help from within invariably invigorates.

-Samuel Smiles

If you are successful, remember that somewhere, sometime, someone gave you a lift or an idea that started you in the right direction. Remember, also, that you are indebted to life until you help some less fortunate person, just as you were helped.

-Anonymous

The return from your work must be the satisfaction which that work brings you and the world's need of that work. With this, life is heaven or as near heaven as you can get. Without this, with work which you despise, which bores you and which the world does not need, this life is hell.

-William Edward Burghardt DuBois

The highest possible stage in moral culture is when we recognize that we ought to control our thoughts.

-Charles Darwin

Aspiration is greater that realization, because it keeps us eternally climbing upward toward some unattained goal.

-Napoleon Hill

It is your work in life that is the ultimate seduction.
-Pablo Picasso

There are some days when I think I am going to die from an overdose of satisfaction.
-Salvador Dali

Nothing contributes so much to tranquilize the mind as a steady purpose, a point on which the soul may fix its intellectual eye.
-Mary Wollstonecraft Shelley

No man achieves great success who is unwilling to make personal sacrifices.
-Anonymous

Do what you can with what you have, with where you are.
-Theodore Roosevelt

We may affirm, absolutely, that nothing great in the world has been accomplished without passion.
-Hegel

The greatest pleasure I know is to do a good action by stealth and to have it found out by accident.

-Charles Lamb

Success is a journey, not a destination.

-Anonymous

So long as we love, we serve; so long as we are loved by others, I would almost say that we are indispensable; and no man is useless while he has a friend.

-Robert Louis Stevenson

One must not lose desires. They are mighty stimulants to creativeness, to love and to long life.

-Alexander Bogomoletz

The secret of success is constancy to purpose.

-Benjamin Disraeli

It is the chiefest point of happiness that a man is willing to be what he is.

-Erasmus

When you get right down to the root of the meaning of the word *succeed,* you find it simply means to follow through.

-F.W. Nichol

Even if you're on the right track, you'll get run over if you just sit there.

-Will Rogers

The destiny of mankind is not decided by material computation. We learn that we are spirits, not animals, and that something is going on in space and time, and beyond space and time, which, whether we like it or not, spells duty.

-Winston S. Churchill

Riches are not from an abundance of worldly goods, but from a contented mind.

-Mohammed

When you have a true desire to play, excelling is no longer work.

-Anonymous

In the valleys, you look for the mountains. In the mountains, you've searched for the rivers. There is nowhere to go. You are where you belong. You can live the life you dreamed.

-Judy Collins

I am thankful for the adversities which have crossed my pathway, for they have taught me tolerance, sympathy, self-control, perseverance and some other virtues I might never have known.

-Napoleon Hill

Lord, make me an instrument of your peace. Where there is hatred, let me sow love; where there is injury, pardon; where there is doubt, faith; where there is despair, hope; where there is darkness, light; and where there is sadness, joy.

-St. Francis of Assisi

Properly, we should read for power. Man reading should be man intensely alive. The book should be a ball of light in one's hand.

-Ezra Pound

Kindness can become its own motive. We are made kind by being kind.

-Eric Hoffer

Every human mind feels pleasure in doing good to another.

-Thomas Jefferson

To hate and to fear is to be psychologically ill. It is, in fact, the consuming illness of our time.

-H.A. Overstreet

The essence of greatness is the ability to choose personal fulfillment in circumstances where others choose madness.

-Anonymous

There is no failure except in no longer trying.

-Elbert Hubbard

What a wonderful life I've had! I only wish I'd realized it sooner.

-Colette

The best investment is in the tools of one's own trade.
-Benjamin Franklin

An investment in knowledge pays the best dividends.
-Anonymous

Faced with the choice between changing one's mind and proving there is no need to do so, almost everyone gets busy on the proof.
-John Kenneth Galbraith

I know I am here. I know I had nothing to do with my coming, and I shall have but little, if anything, to do with my going, therefore I will not worry because worries are of no avail.
-Napoleon Hill

Moderation is the key of lasting enjoyment.
-Hosea Ballou

No man is a failure who is enjoying life.
-William Feather

Do not take life too seriously. You will never get out of it alive.

-Elbert Hubbard

A noble person attracts noble people, and knows how to hold on to them.

-Goethe

The only medicine for suffering, crime and all the other woes of mankind, is wisdom.

-Thomas Henry Huxley

Heavy thoughts bring on physical maladies.

-Martin Luther

Leaders are readers.

-Anonymous

If the essential core of the person is denied or suppressed, he gets sick sometimes in obvious ways, sometimes in subtle ways, sometimes immediately, sometimes later.

-Abraham Maslow

He who has begun is half done. Dare to be wise; begin!
-Horace

Man must evolve for all human conflict a method which rejects revenge, aggression and retaliation. The foundation of such a method is love.
-Martin Luther King Jr.

If at first you don't succeed you're running about average.
-M.H. Alderson

Excellence can be attained if you care more than others think is wise, risk more than others think is safe, dream more than others think is practical, expect more than others think is possible.
-Anonymous

Without this playing with fantasy, no creative work has ever yet come to birth. The debt we owe to the play of imagination is incalculable.
-Carl Jung

By perseverance the snail reached the ark.
-Charles Haddon Spurgeon

If we open a quarrel between the past and the present, we shall find that we have lost the future.
-Winston S. Churchill

The fountain of content must spring up in the mind. He who has so little knowledge of human nature as to see his happiness by changing anything but his own disposition will waste his life in fruitless efforts and multiply the griefs which he proposes to remove.
-Samuel Johnson

Service, Sacrifice and Self-Control are three words which must be well understood by the person who succeeds in doing something that is of help to the world.
-Napoleon Hill

The best thing about the future is that it comes only one day at a time.
-Abraham Lincoln

Pain is inevitable. Suffering is optional.
-M. Kathleen Casey

The concessions of the weak are the concessions of fear.
-Edmund Burke

The secret to living is giving.
-Anonymous

Positive attitudes, optimism, high self-esteem, and outgoing nature, joyousness, and the ability to cope with stress may be the most important basis for continued good health.
-Helen Hayes

When a man blames others for his failures, it's a good idea to credit others with his successes.
-Howard W. Newton

Thinking to get at once all the gold the goose could give, he killed it and opened it only to find nothing.
-Aesop

The best cure for anger is delay.
-Seneca

The price of greatness is responsibility.
-Winston S. Churchill

Yard by yard, life is hard. Inch by inch, life's a cinch.
-Anonymous

As you think, so shall ye be.
-Jesus

If error is corrected whenever it is recognized as such, the path of error is the path of truth.
-Hans Reichenbach

Life teaches us to be less harsh with ourselves and with others.
-Goethe

Hating people is like burning your own house down to get rid of a rat.
-Harry Emerson Fosdick

It takes less time to achieve success when you concentrate your thought and effort on learning a lot about a little and becoming an expert. Focus your attention and effort to acquire the necessary knowledge, know-how and motivation to become an expert and achieve your specific desired objective.

-Anonymous

It is easier to fight for one's principles than to live up to them.

-Alfred Adler

Ah, but a man's reach should exceed his grasp, or what's a heaven for?

-Robert Browning

To become the spectator of one's own life is to escape the suffering of life.

-Oscar Wilde

Dear God, I pray for patience and I want it *right now!*

-Oren Arnold

I can complain because rose bushes have thorns, or rejoice because the thorn bush has a rose. It is all up to me.

-Anonymous

It's good to be just plain happy; it's a little better to know that you're happy. But to understand that you're happy and to know why and how and still be happy, be happy in the being and the knowing. Well, that is beyond happiness, that is bliss.

-Henry Miller

Mirth is like a flash of lightning that breaks through a gloom of clouds and glitters for a moment. Cheerfulness keeps up a kind of daylight in the mind and fills it with a steady and perpetual serenity.

-Joseph Addison

A powerful agent is the right word. Whenever we come upon one of those intensely right words, the resulting effect is physical as well as spiritual and electrically prompt.

-Mark Twain

All that is comes from the mind; it is based on the mind, it is fashioned by the mind.

-The Pali Canon

Together everyone achieves more.

-Anonymous

Neither a lofty degree of intelligence nor imagination nor both together go to the making of genius. Love, love, love, that is the soul of genius.

-Mozart

It is not enough to have a good mind. The main thing is to use it well.

-Rene Descartes

If we really want to live, we'd better start at once to try.
If we don't, it doesn't matter, we'd better start to die.

-W.H. Auden

Paradise is where I am.

-Francois Marie Arouet Voltaire

Can success change the human mechanism so completely between one dawn and another? Can it make one feel taller, more alive, handsomer, uncommonly gifted and indomitably secure with the certainty that this is the way life will always be? It can and it does!

-Moss Hart

There are two days in the week about which and upon which I never worry. Two carefree days, kept sacredly free from fear and apprehension. One of these days is yesterday and the other day I do not worry about is tomorrow.

-Robert Jones Burdette

Temper is what gets most of us into trouble. Pride is what keeps us there.

-Anonymous

One of the greatest leaders who ever lived stated the secret of his leadership in six words, as follows: "Kindness is more powerful than compulsion."

-Napoleon Hill

By means of an image we are often able to hold on to our lost belongings. But it is the desperateness of losing which picks the flowers of memory, binds the bouquet.

-Colette

One word frees us of all the weight and pain of life. That word is *love.*

-Sophocles

The person who gets ahead is the one who does more than is necessary and keeps on doing it.

-Anonymous

Most of the evils in life arise from man's being unable to sit still in a room.

-Blaise Pascal

Remember that when you make an appointment with another person you assume the responsibility of punctuality, and that you have not the right to be a single minute late.

-Napoleon Hill

Don't play for safety. It's the most dangerous thing in the world.

-Hugh Walpole

Always forgive your enemies. Nothing annoys them so much.

-Oscar Wilde

To be wronged or robbed is nothing unless you continue to remember it.

-Confucius

The world has a way of giving what is demanded of it. If you are frightened and look for failure and poverty, you will get them no matter how hard you may try to succeed. Lack of faith in yourself, in what life will do for you, cuts you off from the good things of the world. Expect victory and you make victory.

-Preston Bradley

Every man has the right to risk his own life in order to save it.

-Jean-Jacques Rousseau

If I have the gift of prophecy and can fathom all mysteries and all knowledge, and if I have a faith that can move mountains, but have not love, I am nothing. If I give all I possess to the poor and surrender my body to the flames, but have not love, I gain nothing. Love is patient, love is kind. It does not envy, it does not boast, it is not proud. It is not rude, it is not self-seeking, it is not easily angered, it keeps no record of wrongs. Love does not delight in evil, but rejoices in the truth. It always protects, always trusts, always hopes, always perseveres. Love never fails. And now these three remain: faith, hope and love. But the greatest of these is love.

-Corinthians 13

Just trust yourself, then you will know how to live.

-Goethe

Forgiveness is the key to action and freedom.

-Hannah Arendt

Action is the antidote to despair.

-Joan Baez

One of the greatest pleasures to be derived from wealth in any form is the delight inherent in choosing the proper vocational program for one's life. The child who has toys that will amuse him in all kinds of weather is enjoying the luxuries of life. The man who selects the proper vocation in life has all the luxuries that life can provide.

-Lloyd E. Baugham

If you are distressed by anything external, the pain is not due to the thing itself, but to your estimate of it; and this you have the power to revoke at any moment.

-Marcus Aurelius Antoninus

Is life not a hundred times too short for us to stifle ourselves?

-Friedrich W. Nietzsche

In the choice between changing one's mind and proving there's no need to do so, most people get busy on the proof.

-John Kenneth Galbraith

A merry heart doeth good like a medicine.
-Proverbs 17: 22

Look well to this day! For it is life, the very life of life. In its brief course lie all the verities and realities of your existence: the bliss of growth, the glory of action, the splendor of beauty. For yesterday is but a dream and tomorrow is only a vision. But, today, well lived makes every yesterday a dream of happiness and every tomorrow a vision of hope. Look well, therefore, to this day.
-Anonymous

Each friend represents a world in us, a world possibly not born until they arrive, and it is only by this meeting that a new world is born.
-Anais Nin

Write injuries in dust, benefits in marble.
-Benjamin Franklin

Follow your bliss.
-Joseph Campbell

There are many who are living far below their possibilities because they are continually handing over their individualities to others. Do you want to be a power in the world? Then be yourself. Be true to the highest within your soul and then allow yourself to be governed by no customs or conventionalities or arbitrary man-made rules that are not founded on principle.

-Ralph Waldo Trine

The quality of my life, today, is up to me and no one else. I make good use of it. I make the best of it. I make this day one of: *Success* rather than failure; *Joy* rather than sorrow; *Love* rather than hate; *Satisfaction* rather than frustration; *Laughter* rather than tears. The choice is always mine. I live creatively, enthusiastically and proudly. I live this day to the fullest.

-Anonymous

The only true happiness comes from squandering ourselves for a purpose.

-William Cowper

Men stumble over the truth from time to time, but most pick themselves up and hurry off as if nothing happened.

-Winston S. Churchill

*Sow an act* and you *reap a habit.*
*Sow a habit* and you *reap a character.*
*Sow a character* and you *reap a destiny.*

-Anonymous

Guilt is the source of sorrows, the avenging fiend that follows behind us with whips and strings.

-Nicholas Rowe

Let your intentions create your methods and not the other way around.

-Benjamin Franklin

In every soul there has been deposited the seed of a great future, but that seed will never germinate, much less grow to maturity, except through the rendering of useful service.

-Napoleon Hill

The thing always happens that you really believe in, and the belief in a thing makes it happen.

-Frank Lloyd Wright

People rarely succeed at anything unless they have fun doing it.

-Anonymous

No man has a chance to enjoy permanent success until he begins to look in a mirror for the real cause of all his mistakes.

-Napoleon Hill

Laziness is nothing more than the habit of resting before you get tired.

-Jules Renard

Some people die at twenty-five and aren't buried until they are seventy-five.

-Benjamin Franklin

From error to error, one discovers the entire truth.

-Sigmund Freud

All men should try to learn, before they die, what they are running from, and to, and why.

-James Thurber

Do your work with your whole heart and you will succeed. There's so little competition.

-Elbert Hubbard

While others may sidetrack your ambitions not a few times, remember that discouragement most frequently comes from within.

-Napoleon Hill

Cooperation is doing with a smile what you have to do anyway.

-Anonymous

If you are lonely when you are alone, you are in bad company.

-Jean-Paul Sartre

Getting there isn't half the fun, it's all the fun.

-Robert Townsend

The one unchangeable certainty is that nothing is unchangeable or certain.

-John F. Kennedy

It is my right to be uncommon if I can. I seek opportunity, not security. I do not wish to be a kept citizen, humbled and dulled by having the state look after me. I want to take the calculated risk; to dream and to build; to fail and to succeed. I refuse to barter incentive for a dole. I prefer the challenges of life to the guaranteed existence; the thrill of fulfillment to the calm state of utopia. I will not trade freedom for beneficence nor my dignity for a handout. I will never cower before any master nor bend to any threat. It is my heritage to stand erect, proud and unafraid; to think and act for myself; enjoy the benefits of my creations and to face the world boldly and say, "This I have done." All this is what it means to be an American.

-Anonymous

Luck is what's left over after planning.

-Matilda Lerner

Man was born together all of one piece. It is the kind of world he has fashioned that has torn him apart. A world of folly! A world of falsehood! A world of fear! With the power of faith, let him put himself together again; faith in himself, faith in his fellowman, faith in his destiny, faith in his God. Then and only then will the world be truly together. Then and only then will man find happiness and peace.

-Rabbi Louis Bienstock

It's not the having, it's the getting.

-Elizabeth Taylor

Don't aim at success. The more you aim at it and make it a target, the more you are going to miss it. For success, like happiness, cannot be pursued; it must ensue as the unintended side-effect of one's personal dedication to a course greater than oneself.

-Viktor Frankl

Better to ask twice than to lose your way once.

-Danish Proverb

Not the fruit of experience, but experience itself is the end.

-Walter Pater

We are here on earth to do good to others. What the others are here for, I don't know.

-W.H. Auden

Try not to become a man of success, but rather, try to become a man of value.

-Albert Einstein

They always say that time changes things, but you actually have to change them yourself.

-Andy Warhol

The best way to forget your own problems is to help someone else solve theirs.

-Anonymous

Borrow trouble for yourself, if that's your nature, but don't lend it to your neighbors.

-Rudyard Kipling

When things go wrong, as they sometimes will. When the road you're trudging seems all uphill. When the funds are low and debts are high and you want to smile but you have to sigh. When care is pressing you down a bit, rest if you must, but don't you quit. Life is queer with its twists and turns as everyone of us sometimes learns. And many a fellow turns about when he might have won had he stuck it out. Don't give up though the pace seems slow. You may succeed with another blow. Often the goal is nearer than it seems to a faint and faltering man. Often the struggler has given up when he might have captured the victor's cup. And he learned too late when the night came down, how close he was to the golden crown. Success is failure turned inside out, the silver tint of the clouds of doubt. And you never can tell how close you are. It may be near when it seems afar. So, stick to the fight when you're hardest hit. It's when things seem worst that you must not quit.

-Anonymous

It is in your moments of decision that your destiny is shaped.

-Tony Robbins

Happiness consists in activity: such is the constitution of our nature: it is a running stream, and not a stagnant pool.

-John M. Good

Opportunity is missed by most people because it is dressed in overalls and looks like work.

-Thomas A. Edison

Men are not afraid of things, but of how they view them.

-Epictetus

If you lose the power to laugh, you lose the power to think.

-Clarence Darrow

Wouldn't it be nice to be as sure of anything as some people are of everything?

-Anonymous

I had the blues because I had no shoes, until upon the street, I met a man who had no feet.

-Dale Carnegie

The most valuable gift you can give another is a good example.

-Anonymous

Anyone who out of the goodness of his heart speaks a helpful word, gives a cheering smile, or smooths over a rough place in another's path knows that the delight he feels is so intimate a part of himself that he lives by it. The joy of surmounting obstacles which once seemed unremovable, and pushing the frontier of accomplishment further - what joy is there like unto it? If those who seek happiness would stop one little minute and think, they would see that the delights they already experience are as countless as the grasses at their feet, or the dewdrops sparkling upon the morning flowers.

-Helen Keller

Thus, the sovereign voluntary path to cheerfulness, if your cheerfulness be lost, is to sit up cheerfully and to act and speak as if cheerfulness were already there.

-William James

The richest man in all the world lives in *Happy Valley.* He is rich in values that endure, in things he cannot lose, things that provide him with contentment, sound health, peace of mind and harmony within his soul. Here is an inventory of his riches and how he acquired them:

- I found happiness by helping others to find it.
- I found sound health by living temperately and eating only the food my body requires to maintain itself.
- I hate no man, envy no man, but love and respect all mankind.
- I am engaged in a labor of love with which I mix play generously; therefore, I seldom grow tired.
- I pray daily, not for more riches, but for more wisdom with which to recognize, embrace, and enjoy the great abundance of riches I already possess.
- I speak no name, save only to honor it, and I slander no man for any cause whatsoever.
- I ask no favors of anyone except the privilege of sharing my blessings with all who desire them.

- I am on good terms with my conscience; therefore, it guides me accurately in everything I do.
- I have more material wealth than I need because I am free from greed and covet only those things I can use constructively while I live.
- My wealth comes from those whom I have benefited by sharing my blessings.
- The estate of *Happy Valley* which I own is not taxable. It exists mainly in my own mind, in intangible riches that cannot be assessed for taxation or appropriated except by those who adopt my way of life. I created this estate over a lifetime of effort by observing nature's laws and forming habits to conform with them.

-Napoleon Hill

If you can run a losing race without blaming your loss on someone else, you have bright prospects of success further down the road in life.

-Napoleon Hill

Count your blessings, not your troubles.

-Dale Carnegie

Our main business is not to see what lies dimly at a distance, but to do what lies clearly at hand.

-Thomas Carlyle

A man will find that as he alters his thoughts toward things and other people, things and other people will alter towards him. Let a man radically alter his thoughts, and he will be astonished at the rapid transformation it will effect in the material conditions of his life. Men do not attract that which they want, but that which they are. The divinity that shapes our ends is in ourselves. It is our very self. All that a man achieves is the direct result of his own thoughts. A man can only rise, conquer and achieve by lifting up his thoughts. He can only remain weak and abject and miserable by refusing to lift up his thoughts.

-James L. Allen

It is natural for people to forget to be grateful; so, if we go around expecting gratitude, we are headed straight for a lot of heartaches.

-Dale Carnegie

Heat not a furnace for your foe so hot that it do singe yourself.

-William Shakespeare

We may not be saintly enough to love our enemies, but for the sake of our own health and happiness, let's at least forgive them and forget them.

-George Rona

If we want to find happiness, let's stop thinking about gratitude or ingratitude and give for the inner joy of giving.

-Dale Carnegie

Don't mistake pleasure for happiness. They are a different breed of dog.

-Josh Billings

Time is a master worker that heals the wounds of temporary defeat, and equalizes the inequalities and rights the wrongs of the world. There is nothing *impossible* with time.

-Napoleon Hill

If you cannot do great things yourself, remember that you may do small things in a great way.
-Napoleon Hill

You are beaten to earth? Well, well, what's that? Come up with a smiling face. It's nothing against you to fall down flat. But to lie there, that's disgrace.
-Edmund Cooke

If a man will devote his time to securing facts in an impartial, objective way, his worries will usually evaporate in the light of knowledge.
-Dean Hawkes

If you call him, your Master will hear you. Seven bars on the door will not hold him. Seven fires burning bright only bring him delight. You can live the life you dream.
-Judy Collins

The greatest obstacle to your success is probably you.
-Frank Tyger

If you are pained by external things, it is not they that disturb you, but your own judgement of them. And it is in your power to wipe out that judgement now.

-Marcus Aurelius Antoninus

Is it not strange that we fear most that which never happens? That we destroy our initiative by the fear of defeat, when in reality, defeat is a most useful tonic and should be accepted as such.

-Napoleon Hill

The only man who makes no mistakes is the man who never does anything. Do not be afraid of mistakes providing you do not make the same one twice.

-Theodore Roosevelt

Perseverance is more prevailing than violence. Many things which cannot be overcome when they are together yield themselves up when taken little by little.

-Plutarch

The man who is tenacious of purpose in a rightful cause is not shaken from his firm resolve by the frenzy of his fellow citizens clamoring for what is wrong, or by the tyrant's threatening countenance.

-Horace

All anyone really requires, as capital on which to start a successful career, is a sound mind, a healthy body and a genuine desire to be of as much service as possible to as many people as possible.

-Napoleon Hill

Nothing is so contagious as enthusiasm. It is the real allegory of the tale of Orpheus. It moves stones, it charms brutes. Enthusiasm is the genius of sincerity and truth accomplishes no victories without it.

-Edward George Bulwer-Lytton

It isn't the experience of today that drives men mad. It is the remorse for something that happened yesterday and the dread of what tomorrow may disclose.

-Robert Jones Burdette

Every man should make up his mind that if he expects to succeed, he must give an honest return for the other man's dollar.

-Edward H. Harriman

Destiny is not a matter of chance, it is a matter of choice; it is not a thing to be waited for, it is a thing to be achieved.

-William Jennings Bryan

Creativity can solve almost any problem. The creative act, the defeat of habit by originality, overcomes everything.

-George Lois

You need have no fear of competition from the person who says, "I'm not paid to do this and I'll not do it." He will never be a dangerous competitor for your job. But watch out for the fellow who remains at his work until it is finished and performs a little more than is expected of him, for he may challenge you at the post and pass you at the grandstand.

-Napoleon Hill

Until you have learned to be tolerant with those who do not always agree with you; until you have cultivated the habit of saying some kind word of those whom you do not admire; until you have formed the habit of looking for the good instead of the bad there is in others, you will be neither successful nor happy.

-Napoleon Hill

Set the course of your lives by the three stars: sincerity, courage, unselfishness. From these, flow a host of other virtues. He who follows them and does not seek success will attain the highest type of success, that which lies in the esteem of those among whom he dwells.

-Dr. Monroe E. Deutsch

Everything a man does for himself he takes with him. Everything he does for others he leaves behind.

-Anonymous

## Think You Can!

If you think you are beaten, *you are.*
If you think you dare not, *you don't.*
If you like to win, but you think *you can't,*
it is almost certain *you won't.*

If you think you'll lose, *you're lost.*
For out in the world, we find success begins with a
fellow's will.
It's all in the state of mind.

If you think you are outclassed, *you are.*
You've got to think high to rise.
You've got to be sure of yourself before you ever win a
prize.

Life's battles don't always go to the stronger or faster
man.
But, sooner or later, the man who wins is the man
*Who Thinks He Can*!

-Andrew Carnegie

## The Value of A Smile

- It costs nothing, but creates much.
- It enriches those who receive without impoverishing those who give.
- It happens in a flash and the memory of it sometimes lasts forever.
- None are so rich they can get along without it, and none so poor but are richer for its benefits.
- It creates happiness in the home, fosters goodwill in a business and is the countersign of friends.
- It is rest to the weary, daylight to the discouraged, sunshine to the sad and nature's best antidote for trouble.
- Yes, it cannot be bought, begged, borrowed or stolen for it is something that is no earthly good to anyone until it is given away.
- And if in the course of the day some of your friends should be too tired to give you a smile, why don't you give them one of yours?
- For nobody needs a smile so much as those who have none left to give......SMILE!

-Anonymous

- Be true to yourself.
- Make each day your masterpiece.
- Help others.
- Drink deeply from good books.
- Make friendship a fine art.
- Build a shelter against a rainy day.
- Pray for guidance and give thanks for your blessings every day.

-John Wooden

## Cast of Characters

- *I Won't* is a tramp,
- *I Can't* is a quitter,
- *I Don't Know* is lazy,
- *I Wish I Could* is a wisher,
- *I Might* is waking up,
- *I Will Try* is on his feet,
- *I Can* is on his way,
- *I Will* is at work,
- *I Did* is now the boss.

-Earl Cassel

## Rules for Business Success

- Carefully examine every detail of the business.
- Be prompt.
- Take time to consider and then decide quickly.
- Dare to go forward.
- Bear your trouble patiently.
- Maintain your integrity as a sacred thing.
- Never tell business lies.
- Make no useless acquaintances.
- Never try to appear as something more than you are.
- Pay your debts promptly.
- Learn how to risk your money at the right time.
- Shun strong liquor.
- Employ your time well.
- Do not reckon on chance.
- Be polite to everyone.
- Never be discouraged.
- Work hard and you will succeed.

-Rothschild

- Do more than exist, *live.*
- Do more than touch, *feel.*
- Do more than look, *observe.*
- Do more than read, *absorb.*
- Do more than hear, *listen.*
- Do more than listen, *understand.*
- Do more than think, *ponder.*
- Do more than talk, *say something.*

-John H. Rhoades

## Good Rules To Follow

- Learn to get along with people.
- Learn to exhibit more patience than any other man
- you know.
- Learn to respect other men's ideas and opinions.
- Learn to think problems through to the end.
- Learn to try to put yourself in the other fellow's place.
- Be democratic.
- Be loyal.
- Cultivate cheerfulness.
- Work.

-Harry J. Klingler

## Ten Success Rules

- Put success before amusement.
- Learn something every day.
- Cut free from routine.
- Concentrate on net profits.
- Make your services known.
- Never worry over trifles.
- Shape your decisions quickly.
- Acquire skill and technique.
- Deserve loyalty and cooperation.
- Value character above all.

-Herbert N. Casson

## Optimists' Club Creed

Promise Yourself:

- To be so strong that nothing can disturb your peace of mind.
- To talk health, happiness, prosperity to every person you meet.
- To make all your friends feel that there is something of value in them.
- To look at the sunny side of everything and make your optimism come true.
- To think only the best, to work only for the best, and to expect the best.
- To be just as enthusiastic about the success of others as you are about your own.
- To forget the mistakes of the past and press on to the greater achievements of the future.
- To wear a cheerful countenance at all times and give every living creature you meet a smile.
- To give so much time to the improvement of yourself that you have no time to criticize others.
- To be too large for worry, too noble for anger, too strong for fear, and too happy to permit presence of trouble.

- *Temperance:* Eat not to dullness; drink not to elevation.
- *Silence:* Speak not but what may benefit others or yourself; avoid trifling conversation.
- *Order:* Let all your things have their places; let each part of your business have its time.
- *Resolution:* Resolve to perform what you ought; perform without fail what you resolve.
- *Frugality:* Make no expense but to do good to others or yourself; i.e. waste nothing.
- *Industry:* Lose no time; be always employed in something useful; cut off all unnecessary actions.
- *Sincerity:* Use no hurtful deceit; think innocently and justly; and if you speak, speak accordingly.
- *Justice:* Wrong none by doing injuries or omitting the benefits that are on your duty.
- *Moderation:* Avoid extremes; forbear resenting injuries so much as you think they deserve.
- *Cleanliness:* Tolerate no uncleanness in body, in clothes, or habitation.
- *Tranquillity:* Be not disturbed at trifles or at accidents common or unavoidable.
- *Chastity:* Rarely use venery but for health or offspring, never to dullness, weakness or the injury of your own or another's peace or reputation.
- *Humility:* Imitate Jesus and Socrates.

-Benjamin Franklin

## Foundation Stones

**In building a firm foundation for success, here are a few stones to remember:**

- The wisdom of *preparation.*
- The value of *confidence.*
- The worth of *honesty.*
- The privilege of *working.*
- The discipline of *struggle.*
- The magnetism of *character.*
- The radiance of *health.*
- The forcefulness of *simplicity.*
- The winsomeness of *courtesy.*
- The attractiveness of *modesty.*
- The inspiration of *cleanliness.*
- The satisfaction of *serving.*
- The power of *suggestion.*
- The buoyancy of *enthusiasm.*
- The advantage of *initiative.*
- The virtue of *patience.*
- The rewards of *cooperation.*
- The fruitfulness of *perseverance.*
- The sportsmanship of *losing.*
- The joy of *winning.*

-Rollo C. Hester

## Ten Commandments

- Never put off till tomorrow what you can do today.
- Never trouble another for what you can do yourself.
- Never spend your money before you have earned it.
- Never buy what you do not want because it is cheap.
- Pride costs more than hunger, thirst and cold.
- We seldom report of having eaten too little.
- Nothing is troublesome that we do willingly.
- How much pain evils have cost us that have never happened.
- Take things always by the smooth handle.
- When angry, count to ten before you speak. If very angry, count to a hundred.

-Thomas Jefferson

## 25 Lessons of Life

1) There's no free lunch. Don't feel entitled to anything you don't sweat or struggle for.

2) Set goals and work quietly and systematically toward them.

3) Assign yourself.

4) Never work just for money or for power. They won't save your soul or help you sleep.

5) Don't be afraid of taking risks or being criticized.

6) Take parenting and family life seriously.

7) Remember that your wife is not your mother or your maid, but your partner and friend.

8) Forming families is serious business.

9) Be honest.

## 25 Lessons of Life cont...

10) Remember and help America; remember that in a democratic society the fellowship of race, class and gender.

11) Sell the shadow for the substance.

12) Never give up.

13) Be confident that you can make a difference.

14) Don't ever stop learning.

15) Don't be afraid of hard work or of teaching your children to work.

16) Slow down and live.

17) Choose your friends carefully.

18) Be a can-do, will-try person.

## 25 Lessons of Life cont...

19) Try to live in the present.

20) Use your political and economic power for the community and others less fortunate.

21) Listen for *the sound of the genuine* within yourself and others.

22) You are in charge of your own attitude.

23) Remember your roots, your history and the forebear's shoulders on which you stand.

24) Be reliable. Be faithful. Finish what you start.

25) Always remember that you are never alone.

# About the Author

"Words To Live By" was compiled by human achievement expert, Todd Leigh Mayo. Mr. Mayo has been advising individuals, groups and businesses since 1979 on personal growth, self improvement, motivation, financial and business planning and health management.

After studying business, finance and psychology in Seattle, Washington he became President of the Student Psychology Department at Shoreline College, then the Director of the Human Behavior Center. Mr. Mayo is the Chairman of the Foundation for Human Achievement™.

Mr. Mayo is the President of Pinnacle Financial Advisors. He has worked with many of the world's most successful business leaders, advising them on both financial and personal growth. Mr. Mayo is a noted expert on behavioral finance.

Mr. Mayo is currently the Director of The Center for Self Improvement™, providing workshops, seminars and consulting on an individual and group basis. Programs focus on self improvement, personal growth and achievement.

## About The Center for Self Improvement™

The Center for Self Improvement™ conducts workshops and seminars for groups and businesses, offers private consultations for individuals and provides books, tapes and reports on the following subjects:

- ☞ Self Improvement and Personal Growth
- ☞ Career and Vocational Development
- ☞ Achieving Business Success
- ☞ Achieving Financial Success
- ☞ Improving Relationships
- ☞ Improving Social Skills
- ☞ Improving Health
- ☞ Improving Communication Skills
- ☞ Motivational Training
- ☞ Building Self-Confidence and Self-Esteem
- ☞ Developing Enthusiasm, Optimism & a Positive Attitude
- ☞ Overcoming Obstacles and Barriers to Happiness
- ☞ Eliminating Fears, Doubts and Insecurities
- ☞ Plus many other topics